SPORTING PAGEANT

Other books of the same flavour
by Terence Horsley

SOARING FLIGHT
FISHING FOR TROUT AND SALMON
FISHING AND FLYING

SPORTING PAGEANT

A Gun, a Rifle, and an Aeroplane

By

TERENCE HORSLEY

H. F. & G. WITHERBY, LTD.
5 WARWICK COURT, LONDON

First published 1947

MADE IN GREAT BRITAIN

PRINTED FOR H. F. & G. WITHERBY LTD.
BY THE RIVERSIDE PRESS, EDINBURGH

DEDICATION

I THINK that a man owes his friends for most of the pleasant moments of his life. I certainly owe mine for nearly all those which are recorded in this book. Without them it wouldn't have been conceived, let alone christened under the ægis of a publisher.

It was, I think, somewhere about our second term, Jim, that I discovered you tied fishing flies? We walked about in those days with only one hand in our pockets, and on Thursday nights we were allowed to " brew " in our studies. If I remember rightly, it was my eggs and your fly-dressings that brought us together. Since then, I haven't had much to offer. But it has never prejudiced your hospitality. You will recall some of the occasions in this book, and I hope they are as pleasant memories to you as they are to me.

I never saw my second creditor until I had known him for a number of years. Do you remember the stumbling bungler who almost fell into your gun-pit on that first wild night on the Ness, " Mac " ? You were more than kind to him ; you insisted that he shared your pit, and you showed him where the geese pitched in different slants of wind. After that, we came to recognise each other in the darkness by our voices, and we would shoot together, and shout our good-byes above the roar of the sea. And then one day we met in daylight and you took me down through the marshes and the long reeds twenty miles up the estuary to show me where to shoot the greylags. Never was a man more generous with his great knowledge.

It is fitting that you should come after " Mac," Charles, and the clue to my reason lies in the bend of

5

the river below the pond where the teal live. " Mac "
is a policeman.

You don't know what pleasure you have given me,
and it may be some recompense to you for the memory
of those cold mornings when I routed you out of bed
long before dawn. Neither you nor Bob (whom I
think you know) was ever put out when I invited myself
to your houses, and then added insult to injury by
enticing you out of doors to shoot your game at
unreasonable hours. Thank you, both of you.

Last, but not least, is the friend who invited me
deer-stalking, and then said before the stag was cold,
" I suppose you'll write a book about this." Well,
Harry, I haven't lived up to your challenge, but I've
done my best. I've trailed at your heels across a good
many miles of tough country, and that last day in the
mist has found its way into these pages. I know that
you will receive it with your customary generosity,
and overlook any errors of the printed word, just as
you overlooked those of its author's marksmanship.

To the five of you I dedicate this book, with sincere
gratitude.

ACKNOWLEDGEMENT

For the technical background to the chapters
dealing with the gun and ammunition best adapted to
wildfowling, and for numerous tables in support of
my argument, I wish to acknowledge my indebtedness
to the book which is rightly accepted as the standard
work on the subject—Major Burrard's *The Modern
Shotgun*.

CONTENTS

CHAPTER   PAGE

I. DAWN TO DUSK 11

II. THE WAYS OF THE WILDFOWL 25

III. THE PURSUIT OF THE FOWL 40

IV. THE GUN FOR THE JOB 62

V. MORE ABOUT GUNS 78

VI. SHOOTING STRAIGHT 93

VII. OUR SHOOT 110

VIII. WORKING THE SHOOT 121

IX. PIGEONS 136

X. THE FOREST 144

XI. WITH A RIFLE 167

NOTES 182

LIST OF ILLUSTRATIONS

FACING PAGE

IN THE TWILIGHT OF A WINTER AFTERNOON THE AUTHOR WAITS FOR THE COMING OF THE GREYLAGS . . 16

I FLEW OVER THE MOUTH OF THE RIVER WHERE IT JOINS THE TAY 17

UP THE VALLEY OF THE EARN (TAY IN THE BACKGROUND) 17

MY HIDE WAS BUILT UNDER THE TREE 32

THE GEESE WERE FEEDING IN THE WHITE CIRCLE . . 33

A MYRIAD FLASHES OF WHITE FROM THE WINGS OF NEWLY ARRIVED GEESE 40

THE MOUTH OF THE RIVER SOUTH ESK 40

THE TAY FLOWS INTO THE SEA 40

HERE THE TIDE BORES INLAND FOR THIRTY MILES . . 41

THE POND BY THE SEA 41

THE CULVERT UNDER THE RAILWAY BY WHICH I APPROACHED THE TEAL 48

THE HILL LOCH AFTER THE TREES WERE CUT DOWN . 48

THE BIRD IN THE BACKGROUND IS ABOUT TO STALL ON THE WATER 49

THE ESTUARY OF THE ITHON, BELOVED BY WILD DUCK . 56

A BIG LOCH DIFFICULT TO SHOOT 56

THE GREAT SANDBAR AND THE SWAMPS WEST OF THE FINDHORN 57

THE DORNOCH FIRTH WITH ITS LOW-LYING DUNES AND MARSHES 57

A CASUAL STROLL MAY BE PRODUCTIVE . . . 64

THE DISUSED QUARRY 64

9

FACING PAGE

THE SWAMPY PLACES ABOUT THE MOUTHS OF THE RIVERS   65

THE FINDHORN 80

ROUGH SHOOT 81

THE DEN 96

THIS FLOODED GROUND USUALLY PRODUCED A DUCK OR TWO   97

IF A GUN STOOD WHERE THE WHITE ARROWS ARE MARKED   97

THE ENTRANCE TO THE PASSAGE LEADING TO THE HOLE IN   112
    THE FIELD . . . .

I HAVE LOOKED DOWN UPON THE FOREST . . . 113

THE COUNTRY OF THE RED DEER 128

THE FORMATION BREAKS AS THE GUNNER FIRES . . 129

CHAPTER I

DAWN TO DUSK

ONE day at Christmas time I was flying up the valley of the Earn, between the Ochils and the south-eastern spurs of the Grampians, and saw below me skein after skein of geese on the wing. They were difficult to see against the burnt umbers of the withered heather, the bracken, and the rotting stubble, and there were probably many others which I missed. I thought that there must be a great gathering in the valley, which often happens when the fowl are settled in their winter quarters. It is a place they like, broad and lightly populated. The river floods easily, and although the dykes hold back the water there are swampy patches and miniature lochs when the October rains have done their work, and along the higher ground the earth is rich in cultivation—ideal ground for hungry wildfowl.

I returned the next day, and flew over the mouth of the river where it joins the Tay, and so continued upstream until it slipped into the mountains between Ben Halton and Ben Chonzie. There was a flock feeding in a dark green field at Dupplin and another behind a dyke at Trinity Gask—perhaps a hundred birds in each. They were probably greylags. Two other small skeins swung away as the aircraft overtook them, and a third pursued an unmindful course half a mile to starboard, no doubt on its way back to the estuary after feeding. There were some duck, too, whose wings flickered against the dull silver of the river and caught the eye—among them a swift, closely-packed formation of teal which rose from the cover of an island.

When I turned east and retraced my course I came

low over the confluence of the Earn and the Tay, and
flew on across the flats and the beds of reeds, as tall as
a man, and split by dark, narrow gullies of water.
As darkness falls, or as the tide drives the geese off the
mud, there is a great flight up-river, and when there is
a gale of wind they skim the stiff, singing forest of
stems, and the gunner has his chance. To-day there
were geese here, too. A score of grey-brown backs
lifted sedately from a sand-bar off the village of Errol ;
and in a stubble to the north another hundred were
feeding, looking like a pattern of scattered boulders.
A few minutes later I was a thousand feet over the city
of Dundee, with its trams and buses and crowded
streets.

That night I telephoned a friend who allows me
to take liberties with his sense of hospitality, and once
again I invited myself to stay with him. He lives in
the heart of the goose country.

" Well," he said, when I arrived, " what do you
want to do ? "

I told him about the geese and the duck—of whose
presence he was not altogether ignorant—and he made
a plan for me. It was a tremendous plan, which was
to last from dawn till dusk, and it included a fishing
rod besides a gun. When I heard it, I hoped that
something remarkable might happen—that I would
remember this day for a long time. My only regret
was that he could not accompany me ; his work as a
farmer was merciless in its demands.

" You might have a good day," he said. " I've
shot practically nothing for a couple of years and the
place is undisturbed."

The plan began before dawn the following morning
with a tramp through the darkling pine-woods towards
a hidden loch. It was a few hundred feet above the
level of the river and on the edge of the wilder country
which reaches down into the valley—a narrow little

place some two hundred and fifty yards long, backed by a steep ridge covered with a network of thickets and young trees. I realised that I should be facing this, for beyond it the sun would rise and give me the light I needed. On my own shore there was a tangle of bracken, heavily frosted this morning, and reaching for fifty feet up the sides of a lesser slope.

As I edged up towards the loch a pigeon broke the pre-dawn silence, the hard rattle of its wings among the dry branches startling in its suddenness. Until now I had felt an interloper in this world of sleep. As I breasted the last rise the only sound was the lapping of the ripples and the crack of a frosted stem under my weight. The light of the stars fell into the water, but the steep slopes on either hand overshadowed the surface so I was unable to see what wildfowl were at rest. It mattered little, for it was too dark to shoot.

I felt my way along the shore, shoes breaking through the crust of frost into the marshy ground. As I went, a mutter in the water, followed by the keen swish of driven spray, and then the softer whistle of wings fell on my ears. I stopped, listening, and peered into the sky. But only the unwinking stars looked back, and though I followed the circling and fading sound I saw nothing. Whatever species of wildfowl had been disturbed, they were gone, leaving the purple-black water empty for the coming dawn.

I built a hide from the dead bracken which grew around the foot of a little mountain ash. The stems cut my fingers, and the falling frost crystals caught the first flush of light which was spreading along the ridge. But the exercise kept me warm, and by the time I had finished it was almost light enough to shoot.

There was a breathless quality to the coming flight which communicated itself to my numb fingers. The air seemed to be stretched like wire, its tension ready to be broken in a single exhilarating moment with the whir of wings. I know of no more exciting moments, no more voracious consumer of the seconds as the light spreads across the sky. Already the red stain of dawn outlined the crest in a deepening band, and below me the furrows of the ripple glinted in the dullest silver.

Yet I thought the duck would never come—that the hurricane of wings which I expected would be no more than the figment of an anxious mind, that some other shooter had been this way—perhaps the day before—to warn off the wildfowl. I could have saved my doubts, for that morning such a flight came in across the pine-woods as I had never seen before. They came in the widening flush of day, and continued while the whole sky burst into flame and the sun lifted himself above the horizon. Had I remained hidden in my bracken house, without shooting, there must have been several hundred duck on the loch—more than many of us are destined ever to see on so small a water.

The pochards came first, swiftly, very low up the gully. They flew in the background of the woods and in the shadow of the opposing ridge, some pitching into the water within a few yards of the hide. One pair settled at my feet, so that had I reached out I could have touched them. They flew in—straight and fearless, as though the loch had been deserted since the beginning of time, and a man with a gun was an evil vision of the future. As each flight heralded its approach by the music of its wings, pitching with a splash, without my seeing them, I began to grow desperate. I could see a few bobbing heads on the water, and eventually I was tempted to shoot, feeling that otherwise I might return empty-handed. I fired and missed, and as the explosion echoed in the hills the pochards at my feet rose with a flurry of wings, to be outlined for a brilliant second against the water.

But the gun was empty and the best chance gone. In a moment the loch was silent again, deserted, and the light shining brighter on the ripple. I should have known better than to fire at the small dark heads so dimly seen.

The plan was going awry. Perhaps a hundred pochard had come and gone, and I was still without success. The light was growing apace, and the chances receding. Already it seemed possible that the new-comers would see the white orb of my face through the tracery of the hide. More likely, the flight was almost over.

Then the mallard came. They came in ones and twos and threes and fours, like a gathering flood. Unlike the pochard they flew high, and for a few seconds were silhouetted against the pink clouds before they plunged for the water. Some of them plunged for the last time, pulled crudely out of the sky by my shot. I felt pity for them, though their fall was so fast and the crash of their bodies so final that their end must have been instantaneous. One bird came down from a hundred feet to plug into the bracken on the summit of the ridge. Another broke the branches of the tree over my head. But most of them went on, to climb back again into the sky, and wheel like ambushed soldiers down the path of the wind. I was shooting execrably, unnerved by the excitement, bewildered by the speed of descending flight which buried the birds in the gloom of the opposing hill. But I am glad that it was this way, for wild duck are too fine to fall to indifferent shooting.

When the full light of day had come I crawled stiffly out of the hide, and walked along the lee shore to pick eight mallard in their full winter plumage from the shallow margin. The bird which had crashed into the tree was already in the bag, leaving only the tenth to be collected from the top of the ridge. It was a poor enough result for the chances. But I was content.

I was unable to find the last mallard, so I left it and walked back through the woods, intending to return after breakfast with a dog.

The sight of the duck laid out in the larder had a good effect on my host. He said that it was time he took out his gun and walked again over some of his ground. So, an hour or two later, we set out together for the loch. Once again I walked up through the woods, now no longer cloaked by the mysterious darkness, but noisy with life. A cock pheasant broke from the trees, and rattled its way to safety. I didn't shoot, for we had hoped that a few teal would have flighted, and my host had left me, so that he could come down quietly on the narrow neck. I was to wait at the embankment.

A few minutes later the sound of a shot told me that he had found the birds. Immediately afterwards a bunch of teal streamed over in tight formation. They were flying so fast that I was lucky to get one of them. My companion had another at the opposite end.

We picked up the lost mallard, and left the water for the young plantation which lay behind it. It was not a part of the plan, but there was still time for the walk before lunch. In the plantation we saw that raiders had been at work. The stripped bark of the young trees had only one meaning—roe deer. We had hoped for a pheasant, but the sooner the marauders were dealt with the better, so we quartered the area, and as we slipped among the trees it was pitiful to see how much damage had been done.

Within a few minutes, my host, who was fifty yards away, fired twice, and when I walked over I saw two roe deer, dead, within a stone's-throw of each other. Then when I went back to bring the car—a perilous journey through a bridle-path and over the rough heath beyond it—I shot a jay which broke out of a

In the twilight of a winter afternoon the author waits for the coming of the greylags. He has dug a pit among the dunes which overlook the long reaches of sand where the river meets the sea. When the wind comes out of the south-west with a gale, the grey geese fly low, to pitch as night falls on the foreshore. Other geese pass overhead and move by the coast in the darkness.

I flew over the mouth of the river where it joins the Tay. *See page* 11.

Up the valley of the Earn (Tay in the background). *See page* 11.

thicket. Another villain had paid the price, and I had half a dozen feathers for the making of a fishing fly in which I have a sublime faith. The luck of this day very nearly failed half-way down the bridle-path, when the car tipped on to its outside wheels on the canted slope. Yet it was perhaps magic which saved it from going right over. We packed the deer safely, and were back in time for lunch. The bag was now 10 mallard; 2 teal; 2 roe deer; 1 jay.

By one o'clock a six-inch Ordnance Survey map was spread on a table, and my host was discoursing on the subject of geese. We were looking at a down-river area where the dykes form strange geometrical patterns over the low-lying fields.

" They've been feeding somewhere in this region," he said. " There's a chance that you'll be able to use one of the dykes and come right up to them."

I nodded, and noticed that the route would take me past a little bog by the side of the road, where I thought there might be a snipe. It would be nice to add a snipe to the bag, although how this was to be done with the " magnum " I proposed to use, in conjunction with a three-inch cartridge loaded with BB, wasn't clear. I mentioned the point, and was immediately blessed with the gift of cartridges loaded with fours— the smallest size of shot he could give me for the big gun.

" Now you'll need a fishing rod," said my host. " You'd better take my light spinning rod and the Illingworth—it's got one of these new braided nylon lines, and I'd like you to try it."

The pencil again hovered over the map, and came to rest opposite on a deep curve of the river where there was an island in the elbow.

" You might get a pike just about here," he said. " I had one of eighteen pounds some years ago, and they tell me they are still about."

B

Then he pointed to an alternative place if this should fail—to a still backwater formed by a bed of overgrown shingle which had almost become a separate island.

A few minutes later I set off by car, with three and a half hours of daylight remaining. The afternoon was windless and grey, with a haze about the Ochils, while the backs of the lower slopes merged into indefinite contours of the darkest shades. I took the road down into the broad valley and stopped where it dipped towards the river at a field drain. The little bog was in front of me, silent, deserted, the soft grey light of the afternoon shining in its still water. It wouldn't take two minutes to walk through its rushes.

I climbed the fence and looked down into the boggy marsh within a dozen yards of the road. My foot was still on the bottom wire when a pair of mallard rose noisily from the far side. It was difficult to understand how I had missed seeing them, while their presence at such close quarters to the public road could only be explained by the deserted aspect of the valley.

I shot one of them—an easy shot—and missed its fellow with the second barrel. " A pity about the snipe," I thought.

Not another thing had risen, and the whole flooded area was barely seventy yards long. I walked through it, however, for there was always a chance of a snipe lying close. Again I could have saved my anxieties, for in those few yards I fired five other cartridges, missing with every one but the last. To this, a snipe folded its lovely wings and was duly collected. The day's bag had increased to 11 mallard, 2 teal, 2 roe deer, 1 jay, 1 snipe.

As the last bird was being pushed into the bag a sound caught my ears which seemed frighteningly close. It was the gungling sound made by geese on the feed. I stood and listened, and thankfully realised that in the still afternoon air the sound was being carried towards me on the gentlest of zephyrs. While the geese must have heard my shots, they were probably far enough away not to have been disturbed.

I got back into the car and drove another mile down the road, to where a farm stood on the rising ground, perhaps fifty feet above the level of the river. Here the sound seemed to be so close that I thought for a moment that it must belong to the domestic breed of the farmyard. On the other hand, this was the place where I had seen geese feeding from my aeroplane, and where I should find a sunken track in the hill-side opening on to the level fields. Somewhere down there I ought to see geese.

The problem which presented itself a few minutes later was interesting, and the substance of it can be seen in the photograph facing page 33, which I took from a few hundred feet above the river. Although the picture was recorded during the following summer, when the trees were in leaf, it sets out the lie of the land and illustrates a typical conundrum set so often by wild geese.

An approach down the track, while the gungling sound of the flock grew louder, showed at least a hundred birds grouped about the far side of the field. The problem was how to get within shot.

After studying the ground, I went back up the cutting to the farm and broke out across the cultivated land where I found a fold in the slope. My track is shown by the dotted white line. The first part was easy, although it meant resisting a covey of partridges which rose within shot. So I came to the strip of wood leading to the river, and following this reached the water itself, without suffering any of the sterner realities usually associated with a stalk. It was when I had to leave the river again that I realised the lie of the ground would compel me to crawl up the drain

leading from the flood water shown in the picture.
However, there was only a hundred yards of it, and
though it was cold it wasn't difficult. I felt now that
I was nearing the end of the journey, for a crawl on
hands and knees through the edge of the flood water
brought me to the dyke itself. Yet the hardest part
was to come, for I found that the dyke was so low that
at no place dare I do anything but crawl. I had
already spent the best part of half an hour on my
knees, and the parts were growing tender.

Ten minutes after this I could have wept from
frustration. I was at the corner of the dyke nearest
the river, when the gungling of the geese, which had
never stopped, rose to a crescendo and was followed
by the noisy beating of hundreds of great wings. I
cursed myself for a clumsy fool, and got to my feet.
The whole flock were on the wing, and over at the far
side of the field, at the bottom of the track from where
I had started, I saw a grey figure turned my way. The
disaster was not my fault, as I had thought, but his.
Yet, having crawled so far, I might at least have
approached the farmer in the same humble position,
and begged him to give me one hour . . . just one
hour alone.

Nevertheless, I still showed myself to be incompetent, for I might have had a fair shot had I remained
concealed behind the dyke. As it was, I fired both
barrels into the brown of them from a hundred and
fifty yards, of course without result. To add insult
to injury, a flight of duck rose from the second patch
of flood water (also shown in the photograph) when
my gun was empty.

There was nothing left to do but to go fishing.
So I went down to the bend in the river marked by my
host, and cast out with a silver spoon. In five minutes
I was into a salmon—a big one, which rushed me up
and down the bank where the grass was level and the

going good. Then, as I saw it clearly for the first time, I realised that it was a kelt. The nylon line thereupon had a test which would have flattered its manufacturer. I hauled the fish to the side, caught it round the tail, and grassed it. A moment later it was back in the river, and I was casting out again for my legitimate prey.

When the pool yielded nothing further, I hurried down-stream to the backwater. There was still over an hour of daylight left, and perhaps after all I should yet improve upon the bag. I didn't like the look of the place—but that was because I am no pike fisherman. It was the sort of backwater which a salmon angler would leave alone, though it might be a place where a dry fly and a trout might meet in a receding flood.

Twenty-five yards out, where the backwater joined with the current of the main river, the bait was snatched. Here suddenly I found all the thrill of a fisherman newly into a fish. I played the beast carefully, and in a few minutes landed a small pike. For a moment it had a pocket of the game bag to itself, but only for a moment. A few casts later I was into another fish, and with scant ceremony hauled it also into the bank. It was the twin brother of the first. Although they weighed only three pounds each, they had a wonderfully clean look about them. I had not noticed such a pleasing quality about pike before, and no doubt it was due to the fresh, swift water in which they hunted.

Five minutes later I hooked a third and last pike. There were probably more to be caught in that dark water ; but as I squatted on the bank, prising the barbs of the spoon from its jaws, I heard the cheeping of partridges in the stubble-field behind me. The afternoon was late and the light was fading from the sky. All the quiet colours of the river and the fields were withdrawing into a monotony of soft greys. It

would be dark in less than an hour. If I was to shoot
a partridge I must hurry.

So the rod and the game bag were slung on to my
back, and I took the gun. Partridges in the half-light
with a charge of No. 4 shot were hardly an ideal
combination, but I hadn't gone fifty yards before the
covey rose—four flickering shadows on the grey of the
winter evening. I saw the tail bird clearly for an
instant, and pulled the trigger. It was sixty yards
away, but the magic of the day was working again, and
the bird crumpled. While I was looking for it, a hare
got up at my feet, and I shot that, too.

The bag was heavy, the dusk rapidly closing, and
aching limbs made me think of the glory of hot water
and the benison of a fire. Yet once more the possibilities of the day were manifested—a gaggle of chattering geese passing high overhead, following the course
of the river. And when, in the ultimate light of the
dusk, I saw the wedge-like formation break and circle,
dropping on rigid wings towards the field I had stalked
so unsuccessfully an hour or two before, I decided
that, after all, the last chance was yet to be tried. So
I went after the geese, and came to the dyke, where I
lay full length on the wet grass and eased my pains.
The birds had gone, but others perchance would
follow.

I don't know how long it was, for I had dozed and
lost all count of time, but suddenly I was fully awake,
aware that the air was alive to the beat of wings and the
strident honking of their owners. I rolled over and lay
across the dyke, eyes straining into the darkness. Once
a shadow passed close to me, but was lost before I
could shoot. Now there was a great gungling coming
from the centre of the field, and there was no doubt
that many birds were already on the ground. Reluctantly, I decided that it was useless to remain longer.
The only light left was a dull patch in the west, and the

sounds I heard were coming from the east. Unless a bird flew through that single small area of light during the next few minutes I had no chance at all.

I had already risen to my feet, and hitched the bag and the fishing rod on to my shoulder, when a fresh honking and a rush of near-by wings made me slide forward the safety catch of the gun. I stood still, peering into the patch of light, and a moment later the magic brought me for a single brief second the picture of three geese some forty yards away. I saw the red flame of my gun stab into the darkness, saw a pair of great wings fold, heard the crash, and took a pace forward to retrieve. In that instant there came a second crash, unmistakable in its finality. I had shot two geese with one cartridge.

The bag seemed lighter as I hitched it on to my back with an additional sixteen pounds on board. The walk up the hill to the farm had a measure of rhythm in it as I leaned forward against the load, reliving the high-lights of the day. I was no longer tired. That last shot, with just sufficient time to pull the gun barrels over those shadowy forms, was something I shall always remember. I can see the geese to-day, their wings synchronised like the engines of a bomber, the curve of them suspended, as it were, for a moment against the light. It was the outer bird which had caught my eye, and this one I had covered and killed. That my shot should have also killed the one flying next to it was a sample of fortune which was typical of the day. The cartridges in the gun were the last two given me by my host—the No. 4 shot, which could not have been better adapted to that light and range.

I stood for a moment when I reached the car, listening. From far down the valley the thin honking of another flight carried through the still air. It was a sound of infinite loneliness, and coming out of the darkness, between the earth and the sky, it seemed to belong to neither. The geese on the flat had departed, but they would be back by morning, and if I returned at sun-up I should hear their gungling again as they nibbled at the young grass. A duck squawked from the low ground on my right, and I remembered that there was a mud field below which had recently contained potatoes. Back in the woods I heard the screech of a jay, and the last cry of a rabbit. Then I pressed the self-starter, and the night went out like a light.

Such matters as these, and how they have come about, and to a lesser degree how others may seek them, are the substance of these pages. That day I carried home in the car the eleven mallard, the brace of teal, the two roe deer, the jay, the snipe, the hare, the partridge, the three pike, and two greylag geese. They were not the result of good shooting, but they were themselves good shooting as I interpret the words.

CHAPTER II

THE WAYS OF THE WILDFOWL

IF you have seen the tideway gathered into the dusk until the sandhills and the water grow together, and watched the faint lights spring into being, flashing or riding like felled stars, and then with your ears strained to distinguish between the swish of the distant tide and the swish of the hoped-for wings, and found in these things an eager peace, exciting, all-absorbing, so that even the frost of the night doesn't numb you, then you have the instincts of a wildfowler.

They are instincts which will bring you back again and again to the unpeopled places. Sometimes a gale will lash the white line of the sea into a fluorescent band between the earth and the sky, and the spray will come riding down on the wind to cake on your lips. But you will welcome it.

Sometimes, the ghost of a fog will steal over the flats, dousing the stars one by one, so that you alone of all things that move and breathe hold sovereignty over the wastes. You may grope your way out of your profitless kingdom, but you will not resent it. By marsh, by pool, by flowing river, you will wait and listen, and darkness will seem a part of you.

I used to be afraid of the dark, and more afraid of its sounds, which I did not understand—the sudden whistle of invisible wings, the rustle in the grass, the rattle of a displaced pebble on a river bank, the cracking of a twig; each of them startling and magnified by the isolation of the night. At first, only the voice of the tide and the river are without menace. But gradually the other small sounds which have their place in the dark explain themselves, and man and his kingdom

merge into one. Now you may wait for wildfowl and
and take your reward in something more than the flesh
and feathers of what you shoot. Those birds of lovely
plumage laid out on the frosted ground seem to be the
incidentals of the chase as much as its motive. As
many have found when fishing by night, the sea-trout
in the larder are a lesser memory than the starlit places
from which they came.

We in this land are lucky in possessing the haunts
beloved by wildfowl. I have flown on a winter's day
from the Orkneys to the English Channel and have
seen on the way a hundred signs of them. The barren
stretch from the northern ramparts of Sutherland—
those black crags which plunge their feet into the rip
of the Pentland Firth—are the most exciting of all.
Southward, across the waste of moor and bog, jewelled
by the lochans, the dark heads bob on silvered faces.
I fly low when I come this way, putting a few birds
to flight, but more often leaving them indifferent
to my roaring passage. For mile after mile the wilderness is without a sign of human habitation, a kingdom
whose remoteness seems to be sealed by the half-ring
of mountains in the south, by the frowning brows of
Scaraben, Morven and Ben Griam.

I lift the aircraft over the darkling ranges, and drop
into the waterways of Dornoch, Fleet, and Cromarty,
where the weeping peaks cluster like sorrowing ladies
about the firths. So I cross the Moray, and swing
over the lower country of St. John, over the glittering
sand-bar which stretches from the Culbin dunes almost
into Nairn itself, and fly along the swamps which follow
the tide-line eastwards.

All the way to Edinburgh, and on through the
swift minutes which carry me to England, I see the
haunts of duck and geese, each plain to the casual eye.
The duck have favourite bays for sheltering, places like
the hook of Boddin point where, year after year, I

know I shall find them.   The estuaries and basins, too, give a glimpse of shadowy wings—Findhorn, Ythan, Montrose, and Tay, and the inland lochs may be speckled with them, particularly Lintrathen and Leven. But no catalogue of names will serve as a directory for the wildfowler.   Wherever there is water and seclusion, from Dunnet Head to the Lizard, there, at some moment of the year, the fowl will gather.

Four out of every five which I have shot have been mallard, with teal, pochard, and golden-eye sharing a second place.   Now and again, a widgeon and a tufted duck have come my way, and once a few eider from the sea.   But whatever have been their species, and whether they have been home-bred or were migrants from the northern shores of Europe, they have all shown that untamed spirit of independence with which the wildfowler himself so often has an affinity.   I think that duck, as distinct from geese, are more deeply imbued with the spirit of the lonely places than any other birds within our shores, and sometimes they seem to be more difficult to approach.   A mallard stalked down wind will reveal a sense of smell which will not shame a red deer.

On the shore of Buddon Ness, where the Tay thrusts a sandy arm into the North Sea, I once had carried into my lungs this sense of isolation which is the peculiar property of the fowl, so much that I felt I had become myself a member of the fraternity.

With a companion I had gone down across the dunes to dig a pit beside a brackish marsh where, in the bitter twilight of a hard winter, the duck were finding open water.   Night fell as the pit was finished, and in the glow of the horizon the first mallard swept over the spiky grasses.   But almost as they came a silver breath grew out of the sea and, rolling over the thin line of the tide, advanced in a deathly silence towards us.   It stole the light from the stars, spreading an opaque veil across the crystal sky, and dousing the last of the glowing light. Within ten minutes it seemed as though my companion and I had withdrawn along a tunnel of time, to be left worldless, like spirits newly dead. The duck, too, appeared subject to the atmosphere, for when they came their wings seemed to be without noise and their flight without purpose. They groped, flickering through the night mist, and the stab of our guns was a living red which alone connected us to a world of sanity.

The flight lasted until the mist completely enclosed us. Shooting with an uncanny instinct, my companion collected three mallard. Then neither of us could see even the margin of the water a few yards in front of the pit. A last whir of wings reached our ears, and a moment afterwards the silence was broken again by the splash as the birds pitched. In that second I felt that the duck and ourselves were a united entity in a lost world.

We felt our way out of the dunes, first skirting the marsh by the hard ground until we came to the hummocks of sand and the frosted grass. Tortuously, we made our way back towards a track where we had left the car, and then my companion, walking ahead with a torch, began to guide me towards the world to which we belonged.

It was to the sand-bars beyond these dunes that the grey geese came. Along the tide-line, where the sea gave up its offerings of bleached driftwood, we dug fresh pits each night and waited. There was no telling if the fowl would come, for though the tide and the moon were favourable they often passed us by, and all we would hear would be the distant gaggle of the skeins far up the estuary. I used a child's bicycle horn to call them, and occasionally its raucous note would carry across the water, to be acknowledged by an answering call, and then later there would be a sight of dark wings coming to investigate. Very occasionally we would get a shot.

I hunted them to better purpose in the fields— among the first sproutings of the winter wheat, in the stubble, and on the low-lying fields by the river where the grass was short and dark green. Among them were greylags and pink-feet, sometimes in hundreds.

Each year when I have been in the north I have kept open eyes and ears for their coming. Sometimes I have caught sight of them first from the cockpit of an aeroplane, sometimes from the ground. One frosty night, when the moon flung the roofs of a little Scottish town into uneven silhouette, I was walking home through the cobbled main street when I heard the first geese of that year. They seemed to fly hard against the sky itself, at the very limit of height obtainable by a bird, and their thin honking among the stars was like the voice of the wild itself. The next day I discovered the field in which they were feeding, and began a stalk which was to teach me once again the qualities of the game with which I was dealing.

The field was a green dome rising from the river, and chosen perhaps because it was so difficult to approach without being seen. The lie of the land gave me a single chance—the cover of a shallow fold in an adjoining stubble which led into the safety of a sunken track.

Once in the track, I thought the rest would be easy, for it carved a slice out of the hill, and a fringe of gorse reached to within a gunshot of where a goose stood sentry with her neck strained to the winter sky. So when I slithered into the cutting without disturbing the watcher I counted myself an accomplished stalker. It was when I raised my head above the level of the bank with the gun cocked that I realised how incompetent I was. I was too far down the track—the nearest geese were ninety yards away on the rising ground. The sentry squawked, and within a matter of seconds the whole flock were lifting laboriously into the still, cold air. I was still lying with gun hopefully outstretched by the time that some two hundred greylags were strung out in a black wedge above the valley. They were swinging seawards along the winding ribbon of the river to where it merged in the distance with the estuary. As their wings were gathered into the afternoon, I scrambled to my knees and contemplated the long walk home. More patience and less eagerness would have made the stalk successful.

As the geese arrive, each year, the first sight of them is occasionally sensational. On one day their haunts are without a sign of life. On the next, they are black with the multitudes. On a lovely October morning, as the world was basking in the sunshine of an Indian summer, I cut downwards through the crisp air over the summit of Bishop Hill, to drop fifteen hundred feet to the surface of Loch Leven. I expected to find duck, but was hardly prepared for the sight which I saw from the cockpit window as I circled St. Serf's Island. The whole of its flat green surface, measuring perhaps three hundred yards from end to end and two hundred yards across, suddenly lifted in front of my eyes. It was an astonishing moment, for I had been watching the clusters of duck gathered around its shores, and the movement of the island surface caught my eye when I was not expecting it.

A myriad flashes of white from the wings of newly arrived geese suddenly glanced in the sunlight. It was impossible even to guess how many birds were moving. A thousand—two thousand—any estimate must be a guess, and I can only record that the island was almost screened by their wings within a matter of seconds. A photograph of the occasion is shown on page 40. I pulled back on the stick and shot upwards to a height from which I could watch in safety without charging the wild confusion below. At five hundred feet I saw them create order out of their chaos, circle their sanctuary, and in dozens and scores settle again on the short grass. I was now too far away to be sure of their species, and left them to graze in peace, feeling that it would be unfair to charge again among them, and possibly ruin for some sportsman his chance that night.

The geese were so easy to find from the air, and so easy to approach closely by using superior speed, that it seemed, as I looked down upon them, that the business of obtaining a bird for the larder could never be more than a matter of form. Yet at ground-level the chances during daylight of getting within a quarter of a mile of, say, that island in Loch Leven, or of the sand-bars in the Tay where they often rested in great numbers, were slender. Before and since, I have enjoyed many failures, learning a little from each, and inspired by the successes to push my stalks to the limits of discomfort to get a shot. No doubt the moonlight gunners of the Essex marshes subject themselves to more physical tortures on the desolation of their tide-washed flats than ever I did in the north. But even up here we had our saltings, and on them the moment eventually arrived when I think I approached the southerner's standard of stoicism. It was a moment, at any rate, in which I realised that the man who is determined to get his goose must abandon the rules by which he ordinarily lives, adopting an attitude of mind which allows his physical being to be subjected to any indignity.

Down on these saltings, flat, grey-green, where there was no end and no beginning to the wet land and the horizon over the sea, I crawled down an open field drain to where the pink-feet were feeding. At first it looked as though it was to be an easy approach, for it offered excellent cover, and it was possible to move

along the drain without even wading. Then I came
to a place where the banks had been cut away so that
the cattle could come down to drink. Both sides were
fenced with close-set larch rails sloping into the water
until the bottom rail was submerged. To have crawled
round would have been to show myself to the geese,
now only sixty or seventy yards away. The nearest
bird had its neck rigid to the sky, and no human being
could have escaped that vigilance. The decision to be
made was drastic, but it meant the difference between
a long chance and almost certain success. The water
was four feet deep, and it was cold, a December cold,
which is bitter on the saltings.

I kept my gun out of the water by passing it over
the bottom rail. I myself had to go underneath it,
and I went down with the resolution of despair. The
dive had to be repeated at the second fence five yards
farther on, and I emerged on its farther side with teeth
chattering but my powder dry. There were now only
fifty yards to go, and I waded down the " pow " a foot
at a time until I thought I was opposite the main bunch.
When I raised my head the birds were there, the
nearest only thirty yards away, and herded close
together I couldn't miss, and fired both barrels where
I stood.

Incidents of this kind are memorable. Yet they are
denied by others which show how easy it is to come up
with wildfowl when unarmed. It has always seemed
remarkable, for instance, how little notice they will take
of an aeroplane. One day, through the whirling blades
of the propeller, a small wedge-shaped formation grew
out of the sky and came towards me as I overtook it.
They were geese.

We were both flying at some fifteen hundred feet
up the valley of the Isla, with the glimmering reaches
of the Montrose basin dancing in the sunlight twenty

My hide was built under the tree marked by
the small arrow. The duck flighted from the
direction of the large arrow. *See page* 13.

miles ahead, and the black peaks of Mayar Dreish and Glas Maol on the port beam.

My course was to carry me past the gaggle, at a distance of some two hundred yards, and perhaps one hundred feet above it. As the gap closed, I expected the birds to take fright, so I was surprised to find myself abeam of them, without arousing their slightest interest. I now appreciated that my line of flight was carrying me a little to the east, and so I turned a few degrees and slowed up the aircraft, so that I might fly parallel with the formation. The moment I made the fractional alteration to course the birds detected it, and their leader swung his formation into a steep ninety-degree turn into the mountains.

Since that day I have flown many thousands of miles over the goose country, from the Orkneys to the Forth, and have had the opportunity, which does not come often to the average wildfowler, of watching my quarry from the air. It has simultaneously given me an insight into the reaction of other types of game to the presence of aircraft.

These experiences deny at least one popular belief which was held in the past—that ground game and birds are disturbed by human aviators. So far from them showing fear of it, I have been joined by companies of rooks and gulls while I have been circling in a glider up to cloud base. The birds have observed that their fellow-aeronaut has discovered a rising air current, and have joined him so that they also may enjoy it ; and vice versa, I have flown a glider into a circling ring of soaring birds which have in turn revealed to me the presence of a thermal.

Nor does the change from a silent glider to a loud-voiced aeroplane make much difference, provided the aeroplane maintains its distance. In the case of duck and geese, an altitude of five hundred feet, combined with a steady course, causes no alarm. Birds resting

The geese were feeding in the white circle. The dotted line shows the track of my stalk. See page 19.

C

on the water will remain where they are and it is only by circling below three hundred feet that alarm is taken.

I remember noticing on one lovely October afternoon the great weed-like patches of duck resting on the water off Buddon Ness. Their heads bobbed on the sunlit ripples from the old lightship to the Carnoustie rocks. I flew amongst them on a straight course ten feet above the water, saw the flocks which were immediately ahead burst to right and left, while those at more than a hundred yards on either hand took no notice. It was as though the wildfowl appreciated that this other bird of the air, however noisy, was about its private business and carried no personal threat. Those duck which had, perforce, to get out of the way were back at rest again within thirty seconds.

Not once, but a score of times, I have noted the skeins of geese against the grey sky of the Earn valley, and following them have marked their feeding grounds. And as many times in the fading light of a winter's afternoon, I have overtaken them on their way back to the tide-washed flats. Provided that I held my course and made no hostile move towards them they were never diverted from their own affairs.

Not far from here the country of the red deer lies behind the battlements of the high-tops. In September and October, when there has been the chance of going after a stag, I have swept the corries at a respectable height to locate the herds. They, too, can be marked from the air, and if I am careful to keep a thousand feet above them I have never known them panic. The reconnaissance is, of course, a pure conceit. The stalker knows better than I the wind which will bring deer on to his ground.

The fact is, there is no longer a fear of the aeroplane among the wild. I defy an aviating sportsman to put up a covey of grouse at over two hundred feet, or rouse a hare from its scrape, or a partridge from the stubble, or put an eider duck off the water. From five hundred feet he will not move any other species of duck, although he may, by circling, put the grey geese on the wing until he is gone.

As a generality, I have found that the birds are more shy on the mudflats up the river than when they are on the sea, and still more shy on enclosed inland waters. I could, for instance, get as near as three hundred feet to the geese massed on the Tay estuary. Here the tide bores inland for thirty miles, the shores lined by a forest of tall reeds. When the tide is out the birds rest on the sand-bars, as it rises they are driven in towards the reeds. While they will take little notice of an aircraft, the only way to get near them on the ground is to wait for a wild night when the rising tide coincides with dusk, for then the birds will come in to the shore, or flight up-river close to the reeds. To wait among those man-high grasses, deafened by the orchestra of a gale among a million stems, and then to hear above it the lonely, wild cry of approaching geese is to experience the best in wildfowling.

On the other hand, any attempt to repeat the success with the aid of a motor-boat is foredoomed to failure. Long before a launch can be run in towards one of the sand-bars the fowl are away. It is a circumstance to be recorded with a sense of personal frustration, for we had a flying-boat station near here and two thirty-knot launches for its service, which sometimes found them- selves with special duties up-river.

A wildfowler's punt is, no doubt, the best craft for shooting on the estuaries. While I have never shot in the fens, I think that the boats they use in the north are similar.

I remember one morning, just after daybreak, drifting down the river towards a pale mirror of the sea, all the limpid colours of a washy dawn around us.

Without either speed or effort we were carried by the gentle ebb across the flats to where many of the sea-fraternity were resting. Our punt had low gunwales which were decorated with tufts of grass and short rushes, so that we looked like a floating mudbank, and the sound of our approach was no more than the lapping of the tide on our sides. We dropped down close to the bank and lay prostrate in the punt, my companion with his head between my legs. Forward was the gun, a single-barrelled four-bore, charged with a five-inch brass cartridge as full of black powder and shot as my old companion could cram it. I might have remembered this charge when he whispered that a bunch of teal were lying ahead on our course about two hundred yards away. But I had never fired a four-bore, and the excitement of our silent approach drove every other thought out of my mind. The old man was whispering again, " They'll bunch together before they rise—shoot then, and aim just over their heads."

We were within fifty yards when they drew suddenly together, and within a second I had fired and was dimly conscious of a voice saying, " You've got the lot . . . every danged one ! " My nose was bleeding, my teeth were through my lower lip, and my shoulder felt as though it had been kicked by a horse. And yet afterwards I was bound to admit that it was the only feasible method of shooting after daylight. A rubber pad and a better grip of the gun would, on the next occasion, give me a chance of survival—while the duck themselves would have no chance at all.

Once I used another sort of boat and met with a measure of success. I used to watch the bobbing forms of the eider from the cliffs in the north, and often wondered whether it would be possible to get among them. They always seemed to remain just out of shot, as though they knew to a yard the range of a wildfowler's gun. The solution was a trip in a fishing coble. As I had hoped, the duck took little notice of the boat—it was probably too familiar a sight to be worthy of their suspicion—and I had half a dozen shots for three birds. This was the first and only time I have ever seen eider nearer than a hundred yards.

With the victims safely in the bottom of the boat I had pangs of regret. The beauty of the drake is too splendid to destroy—at any rate by means of a trick. The exquisite white of its plumage more nearly approaches a source of light than anything I have seen, and the blue-green ring round the neck has a luminous quality as though it were vitalised by electric energy. By contrast, the dull brown of the female makes it hard to believe that they belong to the same species. It is a pity that their flavour is not in keeping with their looks. They are to be classed, reluctantly, with the goosander or a cock capercailzie of advanced years.

Immediately south of these cliffs, behind a level beach of shingle, there was a patch of brackish water which taught me something more of the ways of the wildfowl. It almost denied the carelessness of the eider up the coast. The pool rarely froze, and in the hard weather of a wild January the mallard would come in at dusk with the common gulls to seek shelter.

A hundred yards away, and parallel to the shore, ran the railway. It was a busy line, and trains went by at frequent intervals, the glowing fire-box of their engines throwing the smoke into ruby brilliance. A photograph of it is shown on page 41. In spite of the noise and the light and the sparks, the duck would flight in, only delaying their descent for a few seconds if a train happened to be passing. It seems remarkable that wild creatures, which, in the case of the young birds, can have had only a few months of life, should have learned to estimate so quickly the relative dangers to which they are heir. If so much as the glimmer of

a human face showed beside the pond they would not
come down.

Yet the notes which I have recorded, pertaining
essentially to the winter, do not apply in such measure
at other times. The duck, particularly, which breed at
home are like many others of the fraternity of the moors
and field. During the nesting season they obviously
lose their fear of man—or perhaps it is that they gain
a greater measure of courage. I was crossing the moors
one day, to reach a loch which I was proposing to fish,
when I stumbled on a family party of mallard on their
way to the water. The nest had been nearly a quarter
of a mile from the loch, and the duck was shepherding
her ducklings over the rough ground. They stumbled
repeatedly on the uneven surface, so it seemed impossible that all the chicks could survive the journey.
The mother, whom I had forced to the wing, circled
three or four times and then, seeing that this failed to
drive me away, alighted in the heather, and with
pitiful squawks pretended that she had a broken wing.
I allowed her to lead me away from the ducklings,
and then I turned down the hill again towards the
water. By the side of the loch, several other families
had recently arrived. One old lady squawked an
alarm to her brood as I approached, and hurrying
towards her from the edges of the reeds the ducklings
gathered under her protection. Then, swimming at
top speed, they made off up the loch. Often I have
witnessed that amazing pretence of the broken wing,
a mother showing such courage that it is hard to believe
her a member of the shyest race of birds. It is a
pretence that will always fool a dog, and has gone far
to persuading a human being.

Yet I have shot this water in the cold grey days of
winter, and at the sight of a man on the skyline the
surface has been cleared in a few moments, only an
odd mallard sitting close in the long reeds.

Incidents such as these provide warning enough that wildfowling cannot be approached in the same way as partridge or pheasant shooting. The longer I live the stronger I feel that the sport is one of the few remaining within reach which demands much more than the ability to shoot straight. It is full of negative precepts—things you must not do lest the chances melt away before the time is come for applying the positive rules. In no other pastime have I felt so impotent so often, and yet so inspired to match my wits once again with my beloved enemies.

CHAPTER III

THE PURSUIT OF THE FOWL

THERE were six of them—six perky, wideawake little teal—and before I had finished with them I was half-drowned, half-frozen, and entirely without dignity.

The weather was to blame. It had driven the duck out of the hills where the rivers had frozen, and then it had driven them out of the lowlands, as every pool had become solid. Only a few remained along the banks of the swiftest streams. Some had gone to sea, or to the tide-washed flats where they had discovered a meagre diet among the trailing sea-grasses. No doubt a great many more had migrated south to more tolerable conditions—although from the look of the weather chart they had had a long way to go. All Britain was in the grip of the white hand. But these teal remained. I heard about them from a friend after a day spent on the snowbound fields in pursuit of hares.

" There are half a dozen on the little pond on the other side of the railway," he said. " You might like to have a shot at them."

There was a meaning look in his eye, and when I remembered the place I thought I understood him. The photograph on page 48 shows the situation, although the trees must be imagined as stripped of their foliage.

" It's a funny thing," said my friend, " but there's an area of that pond which never freezes. You'll find the birds there." His invitation had sufficient of a challenge about it to be interesting, and I went immediately to prospect the ground. My antics during the next three afternoons were neither dignified nor

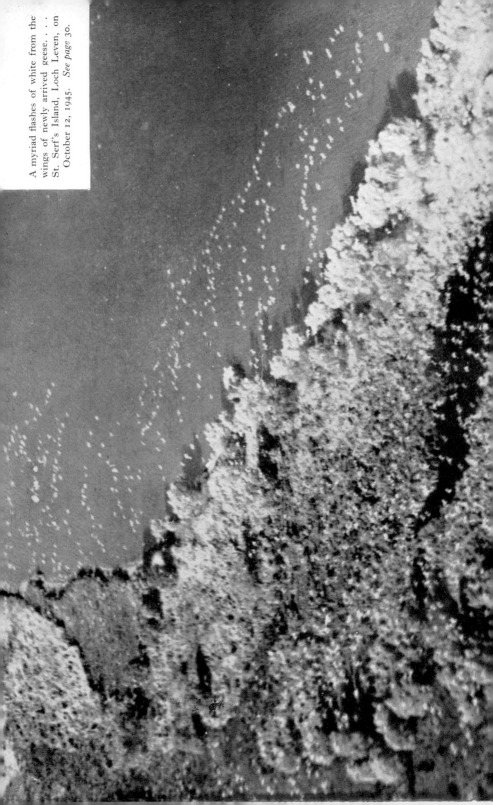

A myriad flashes of white from the wings of newly arrived geese. . . . St. Serf's Island, Loch Leven, on October 12, 1945. *See page* 30.

The mouth of the river South Esk, with Montrose basin and the town of Montrose, a haunt of wildfowl in hard weather.

The Tay flows into the sea.   Buddon Ness is just off the picture to the right.   *See page*

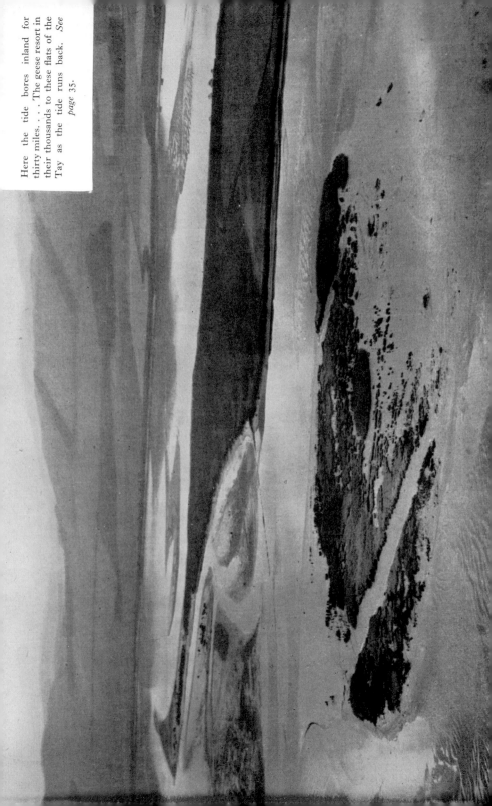

Here the tide bores inland for thirty miles. . . . The geese resort in their thousands to these flats of the Tay as the tide runs back. *See page 35.*

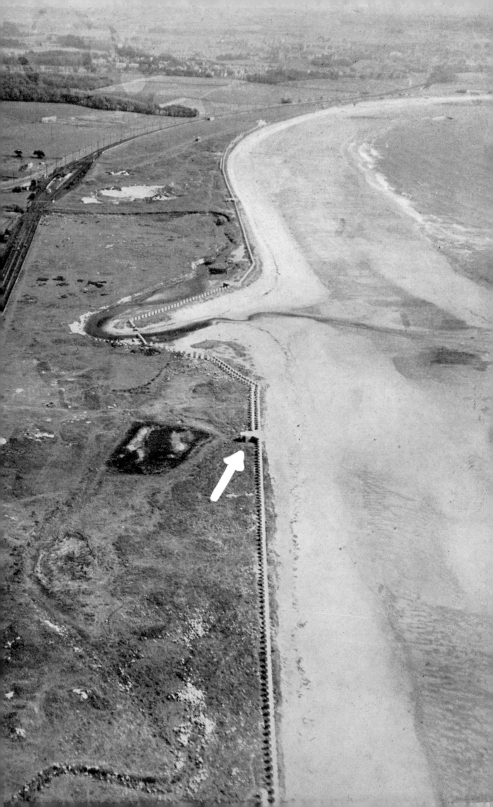

profitable. As will be seen from the picture, the problem was to approach to within shot of the unfrozen part of the pool, which I have marked with blobs of white paint. It might, at first sight, have seemed reasonable to have approached either by the ditch running along the bottom of the railway embankment, or through the trees at the top of the picture. I thought, indeed, that the latter might be possible. They stood on a bluff some twenty feet above the level of the water, and although the ground in between was almost awash, it seemed as though an approach might be made to the water itself by using the scattered bushes as a screen. Thereafter the affair would be in the lap of the gods, for some forty yards of ice-covered surface must still intervene. On the other hand, a light breeze was blowing up the railway, and at least the duck would not have the scent of me. I have known duck accept no more evidence than the smell of a man before they were off, and always they grow restless and watchful at the first hated whiff.

But at this first attempt I chose a third course, and came up the ditch from the left on the opposite side of the embankment ; put up a snipe at the point where the white arrow is painted, and mounted the slope on hands and knees to reach the rails. I crawled along these on my stomach, no doubt looking like a human snow-plough, and saw the teal on the water below me. But they had my scent : for although I remained out of sight, except for a brief second when I raised my head, they moved over to the farthest corner of open water, where they were some seventy yards from the nearest point I could reach.

The arrival of a train halted the proceedings, and I was compelled to roll off the rails while it passed. For a moment the interruption looked as thought it might be prolonged, for the driver slowed down and blew his whistle. Finally, however, he presumed that

The pond by the sea. Arrow denotes concrete pill-box which I used as a hide. *See page 37.*

I was only an eccentric, for I heard him open his steam valve again. When the train had gone, the teal were still clustered at the far corner of the open water, and I was free to resume my journey. I have remarked already on the indifference with which railways and their works are treated by duck.

By the time I arrived opposite the birds my gun barrels were at one with my trousers. They were full of snow. They were duly cleared, and at last I was able to draw a bead on the nearest teal. But even a strong load driving 180 pellets of No. 4 shot is little use against a small duck sitting on water seventy yards away. I was not surprised when the flight took the air without casualties, and when it remained intact after I had sent the shot from the second barrel after them, I felt that it was no more than was to be expected.

The next day I was back at the same place, believing that, after all, the correct approach was from the top of the wooded bluff. The weather held, although to-day there was a slight thaw which detracted from the prospect of a long crawl. I was not, however, destined to mortify my flesh over any great distance. After making certain that the teal had returned, by climbing to the top of the embankment, I made a long circuit to the opposite trees, only to put up the birds through the moving dome of my rear quarters as I crawled from their cover. This second failure provoked all my fighting instincts. It also roused a dormant intelligence, so that I really prospected the pond for the first time. The result was that I found myself staring into the darkness up a culvert, which ran twenty-five feet below the metals and carried the out-flow of the pond into the ditch on the opposite side. There was just room, I thought, for the passage of my body between the top of the water and the roof—provided that it didn't thaw any more. If the passage could be made without my becoming a human bung to the outflow, then I could continue on the further side of the railway with my head above water, right up to the edge of the pond itself. Here I should be within twenty-five yards of my elusive teal—provided always that they had not had enough of my presence already.

I put the plan into operation the next day, but not before donning a pair of breast-high fishing waders, and stopping the barrels of the gun with corks. Both ideas were well-meaning, but before I had passed through five of the twenty-five yards of the culvert I found myself forced into a recumbent position, in which the stream poured into my middle regions by way of my neck. There was, however, no turning back. Apart from the contortion which would have been required, I was determined to shoot one of those teal.

It was a relief to wriggle out into the daylight on the far side, and to know that I should not be discovered a few months later as a tiresome stoppage to the drain. Even lying full length in the stream of melted snow-water was a preferable position to my late attitude inside the culvert.

There was only a score of yards to go, and I covered them against the gentle current in slow time. Every few feet I raised my head with infinite caution above the level of the ditch, to see the teal with their heads tucked neatly beneath their wings. If anybody tells me that teal do not sit with heads under their wings in broad daylight, then I am open to correction. There was sufficient water and mud on my spectacles to make a mistake possible. But, to the best of my knowledge, I got to within twenty-five yards of the birds while every one of them remained fast asleep. The first they heard was the discharge of my gun—happily after I had remembered to remove the corks.

The results were more than discouraging. All the birds woke up with alacrity, and every one of them took off—probably before their eyes were open. It was only after a second despairing shot as they disappeared that the tail bird dropped with a splash into the water.

Such an episode as this can hardly be regarded as orthodox—or most of us would retire from the sport at an early age. But almost every sortie I have made has added to the respect which I feel for the five senses (or should it be six ?) of wild duck. It was possibly a sixth sense which, on a December morning before dawn, warned a bunch of mallard of an approach which seemed impeccable. It was not a disaster that mattered, for the flight which followed was a good one, and as a sample of the orthodox it is worth setting out.

I was moving with a companion up the floor of a gully towards the lower end of a small hill loch—a photograph of it is shown on page 48. There was a heavy cover of trees in those days, Austrian fir and silver spruce, and beside them a track on whose soft surface our feet made no sound. Up the hill-side on either hand the heather deepened into a jungle of its own, heather in need of burning, and neglected like so many other things during these years.

It was a frosty morning, but as yet as dark as pitch, so that even the outline of the slopes which cradled the loch were invisible. In addition, a biting wind was blowing down the gully from the direction of the water, moaning in the trees. It was therefore a surprise to hear the air filled suddenly with a chorus of quacking. Somehow the duck which were already on the loch had detected our presence while we were still a hundred yards away. It could not have been direct vision, for we were below the level of the water, and it would be difficult to believe that we had been scented on so strong a wind coming from the opposite direction. The sound of our feet was left as the only other explanation —a strange one, to say the least of it, with the gentle roar of the trees so persistent above our heads. Yet this day's experience was only an addition to others which led to the same conclusion—that the sense of hearing is as highly developed as scent and sight. Of course, duck will use their voices to call each other, particularly when they are feeding in the open fields at night, but a quacking such as we heard that morning could be interpreted in no other way than as a warning.

We went on up the gully, and while we were still a dozen feet below the level of the loch, and perhaps fifty yards away, the first flight got up. In a moment, a score of birds were in the air, invisible, but noisy as they circled up into the darkness. Soon they were gone and we had the loch to ourselves, once more wrapt in frosty silence.

The first light of dawn was stealing into the sky. The tops of the trees at the head of the gully took on a needle outline, and the shoulders of the enfolding hills grew out of the sky. A cock grouse called, and we knew that it wouldn't be long before the first flight of the morning were on their way. Now the white of the frosted grass which had been so brittle under our feet as we stood on the slope of the embankment reflected the sparkle of the imminent dawn. Behind us the water was taking shape, a pointed triangle, which narrowed three hundred yards away in the rigid spears of a rush bog. The surface held the first glow like a long mirror. Then they came—three of them heralded by the long sweet swish of wings which sent my eyes darting into the sky, picking them up too late, when they were already blurred shapes moving just overhead. We heard the splash on the water as they came down behind us. In this light, and after their battle with the wind up the gully, there was no thought of circling, no attempt to see that the coast was clear before they pitched into the loch. This, I think, was to be expected, for duck are more careless before dawn than they are before dusk, so that even when the wind is light they will come

in after a single circuit, made while they lose height on
rigid wings.

It was a few minutes before the tell-tale swish of
another flight came to us over the trees, and now there
was just sufficient light in the sky to make out their
shapes while a gunshot away. This time they came
over the south end of the embankment, where my
companion was waiting. Neither he nor I were hidden,
but stood openly on the slope, though, had we stood
here in the evening, even with the dark background
of the bank behind us, the chance of a single shot
would have been remote. This second flight came
higher, and I saw the tongue of flame from my companion's gun. At that moment the duck passed into
a line of cloud so that I lost sight of them, but after what
seemed to be an age there was a dull splash far out in
the water behind us. The survivors could be heard
circling higher and higher as they climbed out of
danger.

Now the flights came quickly, only a minute or two
between each. In threes, fours, and less often in
greater numbers, they breasted the tree-tops, to be
outlined against the broadening band of light in the
east. The barrels of my gun soon began to get hot
enough to transmit a little warmth to numb fingers.
Now and again a mallard would crumple overhead and
come down with a heavy splash. A few fell on the
moor to the north side, for several flights sneaked in
round the corner of the wood. In the improving
light they were just visible, even against the bulk of
the mountain.

By half-past eight it was all over. The last flight
had come in against the eastern sky a few minutes
ahead of the sun itself. On the ruffled water the
bodies of the mallard rubbed against the shore,
carried by the wind. We picked up seventeen during
the ensuing half-hour, losing a " diver " through

reluctance to shoot at it on the water, and perhaps one or two others which had made the sanctuary of the long reeds at the head of the loch.

A morning like this is a comparative rarity. I have been more than content to fire a dozen cartridges and pick up three or four birds. But on this occasion I had had twenty-six shots and my companion nearly as many (no great tribute to our accuracy, be it admitted). The conditions were just right ; the duck were plentiful and a strong wind brought them in on a definite line. Moreover the children had been out in the fields on the low ground lifting potatoes. Many had been over-looked. The frost had nipped them, and if there is a titbit beloved by a wild duck it is a rotten potato. They had been feeding during the night, and as the weather was dry there was no convenient flood water to provide the drink upon which every duck seems to insist after feeding. So the conditions conspired to give us a good day. Finally, and this perhaps was most of all in our favour, my host had not been near the loch for a fortnight. No water to which duck flight should be shot more often than once a week, and once a fortnight is a better period. Moreover, the cutting of the wood in the gully had not then begun, and no human being had had occasion to pass that way. Many a fine water has been ruined by the gangs of men who have come to cut down the neighbouring coverts. Their presence during the day has, I am certain, caused duck to look for waters further afield.

One morning twelve months later the chance came to shoot the hill loch again. This time the wind was from the south-east, and was no more than a moderate breeze. It was warmer, and followed a period of floods and gales. The day before I had been out to shoot pheasants on a friend's farm twenty miles away, and we had never seen a bird—a strange circumstance, as

both my host and myself had seen many when we had
walked round only a week before. I now scarcely
expected to do better with the duck, for storms such
as we had have a strange effect on the wild. As we
trudged up to the loch in the darkness it was with no
great hope of repeating the previous year's bag.

It turned out that way, but not for the reason we
had feared. Once again there were plenty of duck, and
they came in threes and fours continuously for half an
hour. On the score of the numbers which flighted
we should have had as many as before. It was a dis-
appointment, but the reason for it is common to many
hill waters. The south-east wind caught the shoulder
of the flanking hill, split it, and created two purely
local winds, which came round the hill and met again
over the loch. Thus it was that as the light strengthened
we saw that the western end was rippled from the west,
while the opposite end, only three hundred yards away,
was rippled from the east. In the middle was a calm.
The effect was bewildering. The birds came in from
all angles, including vertically downwards. They
themselves were nonplussed by the eddies which poured
down from the hills, and one pair landed down wind
within twenty yards of where I crouched among the
spiky reeds on the southern shore. There was a little
light by that time, and it was wonderful to see the fine
airmanship as the mallard sat back on their tails four
feet above the surface. They braked heavily with their
wings, which were set steeply to their line of flight.
(A photograph of a wild swan in identically the same
attitude is shown on page 49. The wings appear
completely stalled, and are being used as air brakes.)

When you are flighting against a dark sky with a
chill layer of stratus cloud blanketing out every hint
of colour from the approaching dawn, it is more
important than ever to face the oncoming flights. It is
impossible to watch more than a small sector of the

The culvert under the railway by which I approached the teal.   *See page* 40.

The Hill Loch after the trees were cut down.   *See page* 44.

The bird in the background is about to stall on the water. Note the use of his webbed feet as air brakes. *See page* 48.

THE PURSUIT OF THE FOWL

sky at once, and even then the available time for raising the gun, swinging it down the line of flight, and firing, cannot be much more than a second. Indeed, I think that a vital requirement for accurate shooting—judging the line of flight—is not fulfilled on many occasions. The shot is more often a snap in which the principal consideration is to pull the trigger before the birds are out of sight. This is, at least, an explanation for poor results on mornings like these. When the conditions are worsened by birds coming in first past one ear and then the other, and then after you have turned round repeating the process from a new direction, it is probably better to acknowledge defeat and go home.

There was, of course, a sitting shot at the mallard which landed on the water in front of me, and I wasn't too proud to draw a bead on them. But the opposite shore-line, barely a hundred yards away, was still dark. Had my companion moved since we had got into position ? If he had, he might now be in my line of fire, and in no mood to receive a bellyful of pellets. Had we made the usual arrangements to signal our movements with a torch, the point would not have arisen. As it was, the duck sitting on the water were reprieved, and with the next ineffectual volley at new arrivals they departed.

Within an hour we were sitting on either side of a log-fire explaining away the reasons for the empty bag. The substance of the inquest has been told, but there was one more factor—night vision. I used to go down to the old flax pond with a man who, when professionally occupied, was a night fighter pilot. While he was not impressive with a shot-gun, he would hiss out a running commentary on targets which were invisible to me. In the service night-vision test he had distinguished himself by getting a " possible." My own score had been twenty-five per cent. of a possible, placing me in a category which qualified me for night flying, but was below the average. It was patent that he was seeing duck twenty or thirty yards farther away than I was. At the hill loch on that disastrous morning the light had been poor enough to require the night-vision side of our eyes—the cells which are known as cones, and which are over a hundred times more sensitive than the cells called rods, which we use by day. The light had been so bad that the rods were useless, and we had both been relying on this secondary sight which gradually takes over its duties as the eye becomes " night adapted." There is no doubt that in the grey half-light before dawn it can play the principal part in shooting. The birds appear as objects which have no focus and no colour, but have movement and direction. The night-vision cones, in fact, detect the target, and draw the day-vision rods towards it for focusing, assessing the range, and firing. Sometimes the day vision is too weak to take up the trail where the night vision leaves off, so that the shadowy object first glimpsed is lost as soon as there is a conscious attempt to focus it. It is because the night cones operate best at an angle of about ten degrees that the link with the day vision often cannot be completed. Proof of it can be had on any fine night, when faint stars can be seen to right and left of the eye's focus point, only to be lost as soon as they are looked at directly. The best proof of all used to be provided in the nights when London's balloon barrage sailed so serenely over the roof-tops. It was usually impossible to spot a balloon except by looking to one side of it.

The man with good night vision undoubtedly " sees " the target several seconds earlier than he who is less blessed. A curious feature of the quality is that it has nothing to do with day vision, and a friend who wears thick spectacles, and is as blind as a bat without them, is brilliant at night. From a pilot's point of view, this same quality has less influence on his abilities

than is imagined, for in coming into a runway at night
he sees nothing of the surface on which he is about to
place his wheels—unless it is lit up by something much
more powerful than the glim-lamps of war-time. He
makes his touch-down through an appreciation of the
decreasing angle between the line of lights and his own
eyes, acquiring an accurate idea of the air space between
his plane and the earth without actually seeing it.

I went out one evening to the flax pond in the hope
of getting a duck at last light. Instead, the evening
developed into a shoot by the light of the moon—a
type of sport which is separate from anything to be
met at dawn or dusk. It was early in the season, and
still and warm—one of those days which seem to have
escaped from the calendar. If it hadn't been for a
heavy day's flying and the urgent desire for quietness
and peace, after the shattering racket of an aircraft
engine, I should not have bothered to ride the few
miles to the cliff-top pond. The moon was well up as
the evening clouds began to dissolve. The water was
a placid mirror holding the soft pink lights of the sky.
It was, indeed, a forlorn chance. When gales roared
out of the east the pond was worth visiting, for then
the duck came up from the sea seeking shelter, and two
or three flights would hurtle in low. In the half-hour
before ultimate darkness half a dozen cartridges often
provided a "roast." But to-night there was not a
single factor favourable to duck-shooting. And yet, as
the moon rose and the light faded out of the west, the
duck began calling to each other from the fields behind
me. Where they had come from I had no way of
knowing, but it was certain enough of where they were
going—down on to the stubble to feed.

I waited awhile beneath the sacking draped among
the branches of the single bush beside the pond, and
still the duck called. They were perhaps three hundred

yards away, somewhere between the sea and me. Before giving up, I tried to call them over by doing some quacking myself. The trick had worked before—and it worked again. By holding the nose and emitting a nasal quack it is possible to produce a fair imitation of the real thing. The important point is not to overdo it and, however lovely the noise may sound, to limit oneself to three or four squawks. Within half a minute the sound of wings could be heard approaching from the east. They swept over my bush, made a hard braking turn, and then just as the bird was about to touch the water I fired. It was a mallard drake. With this bird safely in the bag, hopes rose. After waiting a few minutes I tried the call again, and from across the moonlit fields came an answering quack, but no duck followed it, nor after half an hour did there seem to be any chance of it. The birds were feeding on the stubble.

So I left the hide and started walking towards the sea and the occasional sound of quacking. Two big fields of barley stubble lay together, divided by a stone wall, and as I approached there was a sudden clatter of rising wings within thirty yards. In the next second I must have looked like a tommy-gunner in the jungle searching for an unseen adversary. It was astonishing how, in spite of the bright moonlight, the owners of the wings remained invisible. Reaching downwards in a gentle slope, the smooth surface of the harvested field lay before me. Shadows were cast by a few poles still left standing as protection against the landing of enemy aircraft, and my own shadow was black before me. But never a sign of a duck did I see, although I knew they must be there.

Ten minutes later I was crouched behind the wall dividing the two fields. A dozen or more birds had been put up by my clumsy movements, but they continued to circle unseen overhead, as though determined

to return to the rich feeding below. A flight of three
or four swished on rigid wings immediately overhead
and made a landing some seventy yards away. All I
saw of them was a flickering shadow as they passed.
But very soon my tactics improved, for I began to
discover the elementary rules of wildfowling by moonlight. Now and again a bird would pass across the
face of the moon, and for a fraction of a second its
outline was brilliantly defined. The moment was too
brief to get a shot, even if the gun was held in the
firing position. But before long a thin white cloud
drifted across the face. It looked like an opaque
veil, not merely beautiful, but a background for the
next flight. I hadn't long to wait. The birds which
had been disturbed were ripe for returning and a
flight of three swung low and fast across the cloud.
Watching it, and therefore ready, the first charge of
shot was on its way before the target was lost once
again among the stars. For a moment I was unable to
tell whether the bird was hit, and it seemed a long time
before there came a heavy thud well out in the field.
The sound of that thud made me think of another
occasion when, after a long wait, I had had the chance
of a shot at a pair of geese on the sands of the estuary.
After several seconds of suspense I had made up my
mind that I had missed, when the same kind of heavy
thump reassured me. The delay between pressing
the trigger and hearing a high bird hit the ground is
surprisingly great.

The shot put up most of the duck feeding on the
stubble, and for several minutes they milled around in
the sky overhead in high wide circles. The cloud was
moving away from the moon, but I watched it religiously,
refusing to be tempted by the whistle of wings which
came from other directions and often seemed very close.
The policy paid, for soon I had a second chance and,
as my luck was in, I got yet another bird with the first

barrel. I was so quick this time that I got in another
shot before the targets passed away from the cloud.

Ever since that night I have missed few opportunities of shooting by moonlight. One's technique
improves with practice, even to the extent of seeing
birds which one would have previously missed. The
same improvement has been noticed by night fighter
pilots after constant practice. It is the result of the
brain accepting from the eye the first flicker of evidence
which it transmits. The shadow which is only half
seen is worth shooting at. Success gives one an increasing trust in one's eyes. A night with light clouds,
however, seems to be essential. If the clouds are not
opaque they are merely black, and the task of spotting
the target is hopeless. Nor have I ever succeeded in
shooting either duck or geese against the stars, even
when there is a moon. Men with better night vision
than I no doubt succeed, for it is true that the birds
can be seen under such conditions at short range.

Visits to the flax pond were accompanied by a load
of paraphernalia before we built a permanent hide. It
was transported on a motor-cycle, including any companion who went with me. The principal item was
the hide itself, composed of twelve feet of sacking four
feet wide, which was tacked on to four sharpened poles
at equal intervals. The whole thing rolled up and
went over my shoulder on a sling, together with the
guns, game bags, and the recovery apparatus. This last
was a contraption which owed its invention to one
disastrous night down by the sea, when a mallard drake
was left floating in the centre of the brackish pond
about ten yards from either shore. There was a dead
calm, and the corpse floated serenely out of reach noosed
in the beam of a torch, and yet as far away as though it
were half a mile out to sea. When we tried wading out,
the whole bed of the pond rocked under our feet. It
felt like rotten ice and was more dangerous. We

eventually had to leave the bird where it was, and we
went home and designed what became known as the
" H and C recovery equipment." The substance of
this nonsense was twenty yards of cod-line to which
was tied a disused game bag. The bag was flung across
the corpse, and the whole thing slowly hauled in. Our
aim up to ten yards became deadly, and many a
potential meal was recovered during that bitter winter
of 1941 when the sea-pond alone remained unfrozen.
Had we been able to take a dog on the motor-cycle
as well, the apparatus would have been unnecessary.
My springer spaniel, however, would have nothing to
do with the idea.

As a degree of cunning came with repeated expeditions to every hole which might hold a resting duck,
it was clear that a portable hide was never as effective
as one which was a permanent part of the landscape.
The bush by the flax pond was the first to reach this
desirable state, and, as we improved it, it became the
standard of excellence by which other efforts were
judged. When it was completed it was a human bird's
nest, and when its camouflage was extended to the
shooter wearing a balaclava on his head, and a stocking
over the barrel of his gun, it was a wise duck which
penetrated the disguise.

I have shot from behind brushwood hurdles and
similar contrivances, and from holes dug on the open
shore (spades were often a part of our equipment), and
yet I feel that all these things are inadequate. They
are good in a high wind or during a storm, when the
birds come in low and appear to be less watchful.
But during a calm the hide has to be perfect. On these
nights the birds come in high, perhaps two hundred
feet up, and the first rustle of their wings is only a
preliminary to a wait while they circle, examining every
inch of the ground below. I am certain that a duck
has a sufficiently retentive memory to remember the

point from which it has been shot at before. A human face which is uncovered or the gleam of a gun barrel, or even the whiff of tobacco, is sufficient to give the game away. Often have I seen a flight melt away again into the fading light after such an inspection.

One night a friend telephoned to say that duck were coming in in large numbers to his fields within a few minutes' walk of his house. Unfortunately the moon was on the wane, and didn't rise until the small hours of the morning. The best time for such expeditions is a day or two before a full moon which rises as the sun sets. The light is then continuous, and the moon, low on the horizon, makes a fine background. As an example of this, there was an historic occasion when the same friend shot the same group of fields every night for a week, and the smallest bag was twenty-four birds. This was, of course, exceptional. The lure was a field of potatoes which had never been lifted because of flooding, and night after night the duck kept returning to them in spite of the cannonade.

But, for all the lack of a moon, I decided to try my luck on the following evening. The problem was an interesting one, because it was difficult to decide which of the four fields to watch. At the eastern end of the group was a line of beech-trees, and if you stood with your back to them the whole area fell within view. Whichever field was chosen this was the way the shooter must face, for the last light would come from the sinking sun behind the low hills.

Next to the trees came a big field of oats, which had been flooded by exceptional rains in August and had never been cut. It was now December, and it presented a scene of desolation—a blackened waste, still soggy, and holding swamp-like pools in its centre. However many duck might flight to this storehouse of food within the hour, it was a certainty that at this moment it held a score or more of pheasants. If it hadn't been

The estuary of the Ithon, beloved by wild duck.

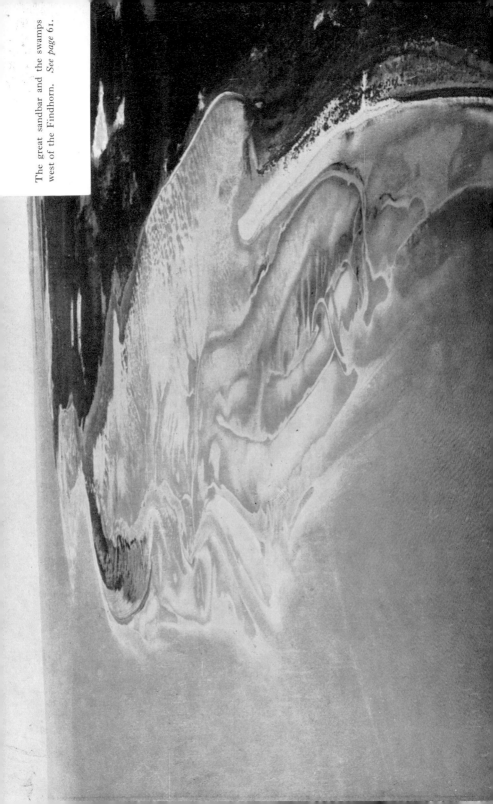

The great sandbar and the swamps west of the Findhorn. *See page 61.*

A big loch difficult to shoot. *See page 59.* The N.W. corner of Loch Lintrathen, which is black with wild-fowl on any winter afternoon.

for the other three fields the choice would have been easy. Over the stone wall on the right was a superb barley stubble, and experience suggests that barley stubble is a strong favourite of the mallard. Then on the other side of the uncut oats was another barley stubble, and in its centre a dozen or more stooks which had sprouted and had never been gathered. These must rank as a great attraction. Lastly, beyond this field again were potatoes—scores of them left on the ground after an inefficient lift. It was this field on which my host was inclined to put his money, in spite of the counter-attractions close by.

It was a cold, frosty evening. The ridges of the muddy lane leading down from the farm had a hard crust and the water in the ruts crackled with newly formed ice. Overhead, the sky was cloudless and the air still, the results of a Polar air stream, and the harbinger of a brilliant starlit night. We discussed the situation as we walked down the lane and decided on a compromise. We would build hides out of the stocks of barley between the uncut oats and the potatoes. This would leave the potatoes immediately ahead in the western light with the oats behind. The idea was that any duck coming in over the beaches and making for the oats would make a wide enough circuit to come within range of the two hides, while we should similarly be on the perimeter of any circuit made over the potato-field ahead. In other words, we thought we could kill three birds with one stone.

It didn't turn out that way. The first sign of a flight was a clear double whistle which probably belonged to some teal. It came from high overhead, but in the fading light it was impossible to see anything. Next my companion caught sight of a few mallard circling the potato-field in the far distance. They didn't settle, but swung round the narrow valley and were lost to view. Thereafter we were reminded that

The Dornoch Firth with its low-lying dunes and marshes. No more lovely resort of wildfowl is to be found in all Scotland.

we were a pair of bungling amateurs. A continuous
quacking broke out at the back of us, and it was obvious
that a large number of duck had crept in unsuspected
and were already down in the uncut oats three hundred
yards away. I tried to quack myself and got an answering call. After a minute or two it was followed by a
swish of wings, but in the dimness of the eastern sky
their owners remained invisible. The quacking continued, and when I could stand it no longer I left the
hide and walked back to the edge of the oat-field.
The only way into it was through its lower corner
under the lee of a spinney, for a big ditch divided the
two fields. As I crossed, a hurricane of wings rose from
near at hand, and then a few more from the centre of
the field where the last light was glinting on a strip of
the flood water. I got up-light under the beech-trees
and made out towards the pool through the tangled
mush of oats. Every few steps a duck would get up
in front of me. If there had been any light I should
have had good shooting. But there wasn't any, and
the birds kept low against the background of the
opposite hedge. I never saw a duck. There seemed to
be some hope of my companion getting a shot, for they
were obviously flying right over his barley stook in the
next field. The silence from his direction was ominous,
and after a few minutes the area was deserted.

This was an example of two people getting amongst
a large number of wildfowl at close range without
either of them having a chance. It was the sort of
failure which is due to the unwise selection of a position.
Had we, in the first place, lined the beech-trees with
the western sky for a background, there would have been
plenty of light by which to shoot when the first duck
dropped down into the oats.

Most of my shooting has been on small waters—
ponds and little lochs, some of them less than half an

acre and few of them more than three or four acres.
They have a great charm, and are the ideal haunts of
the lonely sportsman. Any and every bird which flights
is within shot. Compare this with the human speck
crouched by some mighty sheet of water, probably in
an agony of mind lest he has chosen the wrong place.
It is so easy to make a mistake, and the birds flight in
from all points except the one by which he is waiting.
Yet broad acres are often all that many a wildfowler
knows. His outlook and expectations are different
from mine, although his pleasure may not be less.
There is a lake I know more than a mile long, with
marshes about its shore and some fine timber, and above
it a face of broken crag with a crest of heather. On a
winter's afternoon there may be a thousand duck—
mallard, golden-eye, teal—swimming in the central
mirror as inaccessible as any treasure in a looking-glass.
Approach the shore, and the duck will get up, circle
briefly, and settle at the far end of the water. Wait for
them again at dusk, or before dawn, and, after agonies
of indecision as to the best place to stand, the flights
will come in to the left or right, and you will be lucky
if you get a shot.

But creep softly down the tongue of land at the
western end, following the track between the bushes
and under the trees, to take up a position in one of the
well-built hides, and then wait for the keeper in the boat
to put up the birds—and the results will be very different.
There will be other guns in the hides to right and left,
and as the boat moves up the loch from the far end
the birds will rise, and if the wind is strong they will
come low over your head. This is the only way to shoot
a big water like this—but I doubt whether it compares
for sport with the lesser places.

High up in the hills is another hill loch where I
have fished for trout on many occasions. On a
November night of storm, over a thousand feet above

sea-level, I froze in the lee of a broken wall, looking out on to such a desolation of heather and crag as is to be seen only beyond the heads of the valleys. My reward was a flight of duck which was numbered in scores, a symphony of wild wings, free and lovely to look at against the tattered skyline of mountains. But a couple of shots was all I had. One day I should like to shoot this loch scientifically instead of haphazardly. A companion, a well-built hide, a wait for the right wind, and there might be a chance. But for preference I should never choose a water so wide or so wild. Even though many more birds flight to such a sanctuary, a successful shoot requires something more than the lonely sportsman can bring to it.

I don't think there is a much better chance by the average river. In hard weather the majority of the wildfowl distribute themselves along the banks, but if they have been heavily shot they are so wary that approach to within a hundred yards can only be the result of a well-planned stalk. It is better to enlist a companion, and, starting a mile apart, to walk towards each other. The habit of wildfowl to follow closely the course of the river has its own reward, and if one of the guns remains in hiding the possibilities are even greater. On the other hand, I know of one or two lonely river reaches which have remained undisturbed for long enough for the duck to acquire that sense of security which is the natural property of all wild creatures when left to themselves. If the banks of a river and the adjoining feeding grounds are not shot for a couple of years, the presence of a farming community alone will not inculcate into them the exaggerated caution with which we are so familiar. Under these conditions, a duck will not rise from beneath a bank until the sportsman is within shot, so that even a casual stroll by the river may be productive.

Long ago, when Charles St. John was writing of his

beloved Findhorn and the coast of Moray and Nairn, the wildfowl were probably more plentiful and less easily alarmed. Yet even now these lonely shores, with their sandy flats and pools of flood water, are rich in possibilities. I print two photographs of the St. John country from which it will be seen how ideal was the land over which he shot. The first shows the Findhorn basin (page 80) and the second the great sand-bar, with its inland swamps and pools (page 57). They were taken from a height of a thousand feet.

Further to the west and north is a bold, indented coast, still rich in all things except people. The Moray Firth, looking up towards Inverness, and the Cromarty Firth are wondrous inlets still unspoiled by man. But, of all the quiet places to which the wildfowl come, I know of none which compare in lonely beauty with the silver reaches of the Dornoch Firth, and the little secret loch called "Fleet" to the north of it. One day, armed with a camera, besides more warlike instruments, I took the photograph facing page 57. This is a country which will survive, must survive, the ruthless advance of a civilisation which means death to every wild thing in its path. It represents what I think is in the mind of every duck when it sights our shores on its first winter migration from the north. Here is the emptiness of peace, yet the fullness of life, the silent, silvered Avalons of the bird-world, hedged by mountains, and rich enough in shelter and food to make it an all-in-all to tiring wings. Only when the journey south is continued do the fowl realise that all our Avalons are not the same, while we on our part realise equally that the cunning which they soon acquire must be matched by greater cunning.

CHAPTER IV

THE GUN FOR THE JOB

I HAVE fired a sufficient number of cartridges at wild-fowl to be satisfied in my own mind about the best methods of conducting the preliminaries—of stalking, of building hides, and of taking up a position so as to get a fair shot. But I have never achieved that happy and dogmatic state of mind which enables me with equal confidence to pick out the best gun for the occasion and the right ammunition. One friend goes out with a thirty-two-inch twelve-bore chambered for three-inch cartridges, fully choked in both barrels. Another uses his twenty-eight-inch standard twelve with an improved cylinder and only a half-choke in the left barrel. A third fancies an eight-bore, while a fourth will look at nothing—at any rate when he goes out after geese — save an enormous four-bore. It is a weapon whose five-inch cartridge throws about a quarter of a pound of lead, and its execution among a flock of geese is impressive. Were it not for its enormous weight, its recoil must have made an invalid of him long ago.

I have used all these calibres in a feverish attempt to find an all-purpose weapon. But the ideal gun remains elusive. From the hide at the flax pond, when the light is draining out of the sky, a standard twelve-bore and a $2\frac{1}{2}$-inch cartridge loaded with No. 6 shot is more effective than any other. The birds are killed within the normal range of forty yards and the only consideration is a good thirty-inch pattern. Duck have formed the habit of coming in late here and they cannot be seen at extreme ranges.

But there is a grassy hollow in a fold of the hills not many miles away where the range is rarely less than fifty yards. It is a place where the duck—particularly teal—sit during the daylight hours. They are worth stalking, for often there are a hundred of them in an area little bigger than the back garden of a suburban villa. But the long walk, and the stiff climb at the end of it, give one a feeling that a brace of teal, and perhaps an odd mallard, is the only reasonable reward. But the gully leading up to the depression ends suddenly in a grassy step, and beyond this, for fifty yards, there is not a scrap of cover. More often than not the duck get up as an anxious head peers over the lip, and when that happens the nearest target is sixty yards away by the time the gun has been raised and fired.

The last time I stalked this place, a cloud of teal rose as my companion and I looked over the ridge. The twelve-bore gun I was using, with its standard $2\frac{1}{2}$-inch cartridge and $1\frac{1}{16}$th oz. of No. 4 shot, was operating at its extreme range. I fired both barrels in quick succession into the middle of the cloud, and when two birds dropped from the massive formation I knew I had luck alone to thank. The pattern of No. 4 shot at sixty yards, even from the half-choke of the left barrel, contained a mere 55 pellets in the thirty-inch circle, and it has been reliably estimated that at least 145 pellets are needed in the pattern to be certain of hitting a bird of this size in a vital place.

On the other hand, my companion, who was using a 32-inch twelve-bore with three-inch cartridges, took a deliberate right and left, and followed this up by killing a mallard, rising later than the teal, at a range which we subsequently paced out at seventy-eight yards. I myself did not fire, for the bird was patently beyond the capabilites of the gun.

A few casual experiences of this kind make one an enthusiast for the heavier weapon, and where geese are concerned a gun bored to a full choke of forty-thousandths of an inch, coupled with a three-inch low-velocity cartridge and 1¾ oz. of BB shot, is undoubtedly a potent weapon. I once became so enthusiastic for such a gun that I took it duck-shooting on every possible occasion, often when its special characteristics were a disadvantage. I was finally cured of its spell one afternoon along a deserted stretch of river. The duck were lying close under the bank on my own side and I found myself with frequent shots of between twenty-five and thirty yards—a range upon which most shooters would have backed their chances. I think that on every single occasion I missed with the first barrel, and missed again with an unwarrantable proportion of second attempts. At first, I thought I was shooting badly. But when a bird hit at fifty yards fell into the river I was soon reminded of the truth. It was winged, and as the current carried it towards me I fired at it again at about twenty-five yards. The almost unbelievably narrow circle of the shot as they hit the water made it clear why I had been missing the birds on the wing—as I now missed this one in the river.

The diameter of the spread was actually about twenty inches, which was leaving too little room for sighting error in the hands of an ordinary shooter. Such a spread might suit a first-class shot, provided that he did not object to his game being well ballasted with lead. But for most of us this gun could only be said to be an effective weapon at ranges of over thirty-five yards—with a limit of sixty yards when using up to No. 5 shot. The total spread at sixty yards is in the region of six feet, at which range there is still a sufficient concentration of pellets with a thirty-inch circle to make a shot a fair gamble. At the same time, it has

A casual stroll may be productive. *See page* 60.

...he disused quarry with its surrounding scrub offers ideal cover for game. *See page* 115.

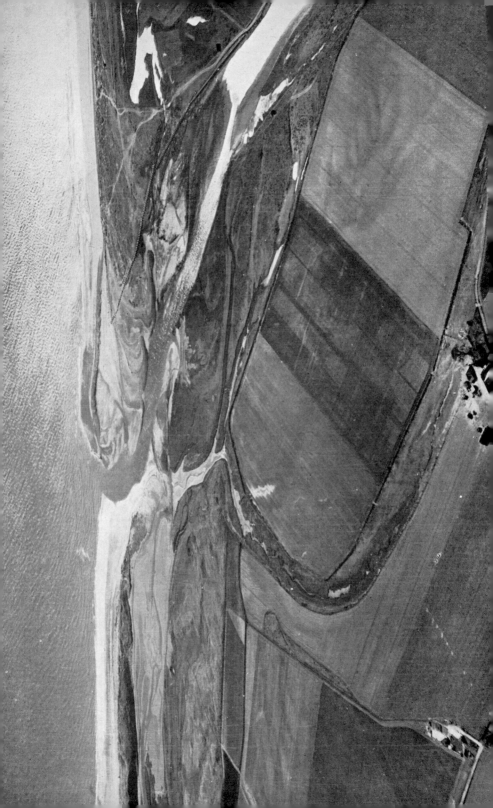

to be remembered that only small shot will provide an adequate density of pattern at long distances, and this immediately involves the question of whether they will retain sufficient velocity to kill. This is a point which will be discussed in a moment. But in the meantime, let us recognise that a three-inch cartridge seems, at first sight, to be ideal ammunition. If used in conjunction with a full choke it will put 140 pellets of No. 6 into the thirty-inch circle at sixty yards or 100 pellets of No. 4.

Yet it was this weapon, once mentally classed as infallible, which eventually demonstrated the limitations of even the best-adapted shot-guns. I thought that I had acquired something which would kill at anything up to eighty yards with No. 4 shot as often as it was held straight. I was like other shooters who place a sublime faith in their weapons, believing more in their efficiency than in their own capabilities. The sooner the positions are reversed the better, and the more likely is the right gun and ammunition to be chosen for the class of sport to be expected. More important still, one will soon be led to an understanding of what the gun will not do. As soon as the problem is considered objectively, and the experience of a few lucky shots disregarded, basic factors become plain.

First, the nature of the wildfowl prescribes that the gun should be effective at extreme ranges. That is the outstanding requirement which a single season on the marshes must demonstrate.

Unfortunately the word effective embraces so many dependent considerations that a mere recommendation to a large gun with a large cartridge is meaningless. On the other hand, the problem can be reduced to simple mathematics, and if these are considered in their logical sequence the wildfowler must be led towards the right decisions. Placed in order of

E

The swampy places about the mouths of the rivers are favourite places of the fowl. The river North Esk.

importance, the factors of principal influence must be the following :

1. The shot must have sufficient velocity when they hit the target to penetrate and kill.
2. The pattern of the shot must be sufficiently dense to discount the possibility of the bird flying through it.
3. The gun must be suitable to take the cartridge which will fulfil the first two conditions, and combine with it to produce the predetermined results.

If these conditions are satisfied for any given range, the bird must die if the shooting is straight. The secondary considerations can, for the moment, be ignored. They are the outcome of the first, and determine the weight of the gun and the recoil. While they are matters of importance to one's individual physical limitations, they are not the deciding factors.

Perhaps the most surprising item of information which comes to the casual inquirer is that the shot from a standard twelve-bore cartridge which is fired from the standard gun would scarcely reach the height of the Nelson Column if it was fired straight into the air. This is for No. 6 shot, which is probably the most effective for general game, and with many people the most popular. The same size of shot will travel just over two hundred yards when the gun is held at the most favourable angle for extreme range. These two facts are a reminder of the limited carrying power of ordinary ammunition. They are in startling contrast to the performance of a rifle, and even bear no relation to the lethal range of ball when fired from the same gun with the same quantity of powder. To test this, I have fired a number of cartridges loaded with ball at a wooden target composed of five thicknesses of $\frac{3}{4}$-inch floor-boarding bolted together. The range was eighty yards, and the ball went through the target and disappeared into the earth bank on the far side. When SG was used, of which there are nine pellets in the standard cartridge, three thicknesses of board were penetrated. On the other hand, No. 6 size shot made no more than a number of light punctures. The same shot hitting a strong bird well protected by feathers was obviously not lethal at this range.

One or two amateur experiments of this kind soon arouse in the mind a demand to know what the various classes of ammunition will do, and a brief study of the subject is repaid in the field.

·I have referred to the standard twelve-bore cartridge, and this should be considered first before discussing the longer ammunition. The standard cartridge, then, is reckoned as a $2\frac{1}{2}$-inch paper case loaded with $1\frac{1}{16}$th oz. of No. 6 shot propelled by thirty-three grains of smokeless diamond powder. It is the cartridge which the gunmaker will probably supply if you send in your order without any specifications other than size of pellet.

Its observed velocity, which is the velocity of the pellets measured over the first twenty yards, is 1050 feet per second. This method of measuring is an arbitrary one, and is considered to be the most convenient. Its relationship to the muzzle velocity varies with the size of the shot—because the smaller the pellet the more rapid is its loss of speed, a point demonstrated in the following table :

Size of Shot	Muzzle Velocity	Velocity at 20 yds.	At 60 yds.
BB	1170 f.s.	925 f.s.	605 f.s.
4	1230 ,,	890 ,,	490 ,,
6	1270 ,,	870 ,,	425 ,,
9	1370 ,,	830 ,,	305 ,,

Each of these sizes of shot will give a mean velocity over twenty yards of approximately 1050 feet per second.

The question which immediately arises is at what point has the pellet lost so much speed that it will fail to kill. If we know this, then we know the limit of its range. The answer is that both BB and fours remain lethal at sixty yards, but that sixes and nines fade out respectively at fifty-five and twenty-eight yards. The surprising drop in the killing power between sixes and nines shows how greatly the resistance of the air affects the smaller sizes of shot. To carry the investigation a stage further, it is computed that the extreme ranges for the intermediate sizes are as follows :

No. 6½	50 yards
No. 7	45 yards
No. 8	37 yards

The resistance of the air is not, of course, the sole reason for the diminishing hitting power. The weight of the pellet is an equally important contributor. For instance, a BB pellet travelling at 600 feet per second will have a striking velocity of more than 5 foot-pounds. With a standard charge, this represents its speed at about sixty yards, and it is of interest to note that only ·8 foot-pounds is reckoned sufficient for a kill. No. 4 shot, on the other hand, carries a smaller punch at the same velocity—about 2 foot-pounds— and owing to air resistance it has fallen to this speed after about forty-seven yards.

In the case of sixes and nines, the hitting power has deteriorated still further, although in each instance the pellets are still travelling at 600 feet per second. For sixes the figure is about 1·25 foot-pounds, and for nines, ·6 foot-pounds. In the standard cartridge, the respective ranges at which the pellets will have fallen to this speed are about forty-three and thirty-five yards.

At this stage, it is worth setting out a table for each

of the smaller sizes of shot, so that we can see at a
glance the distance over which it will hold the velocity
required to produce the minimum killing energy of
·8 foot-pounds :

$5\frac{1}{2}$	60 yards
6	55 yards
7	45 yards
8	35 yards
9	28 yards

There can hardly be a shooter who, looking at these
figures, will not plead guilty to firing at game out of
range. They will also recall numerous instances when
the object at which they fired was killed—proving that
the tables are wrong. The truth, of course, is that a
strike in the head can be fatal when the energy contained
in the flying pellet is much less. Alternatively, small
birds, such as snipe, may be penetrated, or equally will
succumb to the shock effect of a strike more readily
than large birds such as geese. These points will recur
later. In the meantime, if the tables are accepted at
their face-value, it is clear that the standard cartridge
has a very limited performance.

Now it is possible to obtain a high-velocity loading
which will give slightly improved results. For practical
purposes, the limit is about 1150 feet per second
observed velocity. Unfortunately, the extra 100 feet
per second makes very little difference at extreme
ranges, while its disadvantages, which will be referred
to later, are such that it is hardly worth while. By
the time a No. 6 pellet has travelled sixty yards it has
lost all but 25 feet per second of the original extra
100 feet per second. It still does not bring this size of
shot into the sixty yards limit, while in the case of No. 7
shot it gives an extra three or four yards only. The high-
velocity complex is a bad one for a shooter to acquire.

The extreme limits of range for the larger sizes of
pellet are clearly shown in the ensuing table. The

figures, of course, do not pay any regard to the pattern,
but they do demonstrate the distance at which a pellet
may be regarded as lethal if it happens to score a hit.
In the first column, the results are shown for a high-
velocity loading. The small difference between this
and the standard load will be duly remarked.

RANGE AT WHICH STRIKING ENERGY FALLS TO
·8 FOOT-POUNDS

Size of Shot	Range in Yards	
	For O.V. of 1150 f.s.	For O.V. of 1050 f.s.
BB	133	128
B	124	118
1	110	105
2	99	94
3	90	85
4	80	76
4½	72	68
5	68	64
5½	63	60

The wildfowler who reaches this stage of his in-
quiries can now say that he has disposed of his chief
velocity problems ; for, regardless of the bore of his
gun and the manner in which it is chambered and
choked, the velocity tables will hold roughly good for
any length and size of cartridge. But before trying to
establish the qualities of the gun which is to fire the
cartridge it will be advisable to answer a big question
which must arise in every shooter's mind. Why cannot
the velocity be so increased that even small shot will
be travelling fast enough at fifty yards and over to kill ?
One remembers that a ·303 rifle bullet can be propelled
out of the muzzle at 3000 feet per second, that an aircraft cannon-shell is moving at over 2500 f.s., a shell

from a big naval gun at over 2250 f.s., and even a heavy bomb dropped from 10,000 feet at about 2000 f.s. By comparison, the velocity of the fastest shot-gun cartridges is very low.

The answer is threefold. Most important of all, perhaps, is the well-established fact that a high velocity has a disastrous effect on the shot pattern. It would be almost true to say that in extreme cases it scatters it all over the countryside. Even with an observed velocity of 1150 f.s. the spread is so wide that a fully choked barrel is desirable to counteract it. Countless experiments have been made to get over the problem, but in every case where velocities have been substantially increased the pattern has deteriorated so as to make it useless for practical purposes.

This disadvantage is sufficient in itself to render further consideration abortive. But, for the sake of driving the argument home, it may be mentioned that the energy required to propel a charge of shot down the barrel at the greatly increased speed to make any appreciable difference at fifty yards has a dramatic effect on the recoil of the gun. There is a limit to the amount of " kick " which an ordinary mortal can stand, and it is for this reason that high-velocity cartridges which are to be fired out of a standard game gun are often filled with a reduced charge of shot in order to bring the recoil once again within tolerable limits. Instead of using $1\frac{1}{16}$th oz. of shot, for instance, such cartridges are often reduced to 1 oz. As soon as this is done, the available number of pellets to complete a pattern at extreme range is fewer and the elements of a vicious circle are complete.

The alternative, of course, is to increase the weight of the gun. The logical development of this is the twelve-bore chambered for three-inch cartridges weighing about 8 lbs. instead of the customary 6 to $6\frac{1}{2}$ lbs. or, carried a stage further, one might use a ten-bore gun weighing 9 lbs. or even an eight-bore weighing 14 lbs. The merits of such weapons certainly have something to recommend them for wildfowling, and their advantages will be mentioned later. In the meantime, let us look at the patterns which are obtainable, for it is through a study of these that a final decision will be reached. The velocity of the pellets has already been shown as sufficient to be lethal at sixty yards for shot down to No. 5½. It looks at first sight, therefore, that a standard 2½-inch cartridge is not such poor ammunition after all. Unfortunately this is not true ; for, apart from the thinness of the pattern, the deterioration of its size and shape is unpredictable after about fifty yards. It cannot, in fact, be relied upon. At the same time, I indicated earlier that a specific number of pellets might be expected at the sixty-yards range, and for what the figures are worth I quote them below, so that one may see what may be expected of them. They are based upon a relative efficiency of about 45 per cent. of the results obtained at forty yards.

Improved Cylinder	Half-Choke	Full Choke
No. 4. 40 pellets	55	65
No. 5½. 60 pellets	75	85

Against this table may be set the number of pellets which are considered necessary to be inside a thirty-inch pattern to kill (for certain) some of the common varieties of game.

Cock pheasant . . .	60
Mallard	70
Hen pheasant	80
Grouse ⎫ Partridge ⎬ . . . Wood-pigeon ⎭	130
Teal ⎫ Woodcock ⎭ . . .	145
Snipe	290

Indeed it must be growing increasingly obvious that a satisfactory pattern and adequate killing energy cannot be combined in a standard cartridge at sixty yards, regardless of the boring of the gun. The best that one can say is that a full choke and a load of No. 5½ shot retain the minimum velocity and pattern to make sure of the first three birds in the list, but not the last six. The wisest conclusion is that sixty yards is too great a range for the standard gun and cartridge for ordinary small game—a conclusion which is driven home by the rapid deterioration in the pattern after fifty yards. It may therefore be best to dismiss the hope of reliable shooting at sixty yards with a standard gun, and try to readjust one's ideas to the shorter range of forty yards. One may be at least certain of consistent results at this distance, for the tables show that the killing energy of all sizes of shot down to sevens remains adequate, while the ordinary half-choke of the left barrel will put 170 pellets of the latter size into the magic circle. Under these conditions all the birds in the list are dead birds—with the exception of snipe.

We must, however, still seek for effect at greater ranges, knowing that quite half the chances we are likely to have at wildfowl will be lost unless we find a solution.

If the argument has been followed, it will then be agreed that a load greater than $1\frac{1}{16}$th oz. is necessary to produce a satisfactory pattern. This means plainly that a special gun is advisable, and a special gun means added weight if the recoil is to be kept within tolerable limits. I have already mentioned the magnum—or the twelve-bore chambered for three-inch ammunition. This is, of course, a heavy gun built to withstand the higher gas pressures of the longer ammunition. It is a possible wildfowler's choice, although not the only one.

The three-inch cartridge loaded with a powder of standard velocity is well able to cope with $1\frac{5}{16}$ oz. of

No. $5\frac{1}{2}$ shot, and if the gun is fully choked in both
barrels the pattern density at forty yards is increased
from 180 to 220, and at sixty yards (in round figures)
from 85 to 105. This is a substantial gain, although it
still fails to make sure of the elusive little teal. It may be
better still to go to a 42-grain bulk powder which will
satisfactorily handle $1\frac{1}{2}$ oz. of No. $5\frac{1}{2}$. The density of
the pattern at forty yards is now increased to 250, and
at sixty yards to about 120. With these cartridges a
larger size of shot, with its increased killing power, is
an obvious choice for mallard. No. $5\frac{1}{2}$ must always be
dangerously light at extreme ranges, and every advantage is to be gained by using a bigger shot if the considerations of pattern will allow it. The $1\frac{1}{2}$ oz. of
No. 4 will provide 180 pellets in the circle at forty
yards (on a full choke) and perhaps 130–140 at sixty
yards. Taken all round, this might be a very good
combination of gun and cartridge for general duck-
shooting where close ranges are not expected. It is
unfortunate that the latter proviso is necessary. But
experience as well as theory shows that the narrow
spread of shot up to thirty yards makes it far too easy
to score a clean miss.

As an alternative to the long-chambered twelve-
bore, a standard ten-bore firing $1\frac{1}{2}$ oz. of shot will
achieve the same results. A ten can furthermore be
chambered for $3\frac{1}{4}$-inch cartridges taking $2\frac{1}{4}$ oz. of large
shot for bigger game, while an eight-bore will fling
over 3 oz. when required. But because the weight of
the gun is directly dependent on the weight of the
charge to be fired, such weapons are a grievous burden
to carry around. They are, perhaps, better adapted to
geese, where 3 oz. of BB, consisting of 210 pellets, are
lethal at well over one hundred yards. One does not
set off for a long day's shooting with such a gun,
and a single shot is possibly the only expenditure of
ammunition to be contemplated.

Personally, I would sooner possess a twelve-bore chambered for three-inch cartridges with a full choke in both barrels, and when it was employed against geese using a low-velocity ammunition firing 2 oz. of BB. The sacrifice of velocity for extra shot space is no disadvantage with big pellets. An observed velocity of 900 feet per second is probably adequate for BB at all practical ranges. A gun of this nature, weighing $7\frac{3}{4}$ lb., is still a possible load to carry about on a hard day's shooting. This latter assertion may be questioned by slightly built sportsmen and it is a point which must, of course, be settled by the individual.

If this chapter opened in a spirit of high hope for discovering a weapon which was practical at a range of eighty yards, it will now be seen that such optimism was unjustified. The conclusion is that the maximum range of even a special gun like a magnum is in the region of sixty yards, while the twelve-bore gun, weighing between 6 and $6\frac{1}{2}$ lb., chambered to fire the standard cartridge is not a long way behind it. The difference is so slight—a matter of perhaps ten yards—that many sportsmen will prefer its more pleasant shooting qualities. Moreover, it will not only save them buying a special gun, but it will not reveal the embarrassing disadvantage of shooting too close a pattern at normal ranges. If the idea of shooting teal at sixty yards must be abandoned, it is at least possible to bring down a mallard with reasonable certainty at this range. I think, therefore, that the choice lies between a standard twelve-bore which is fitted with an improved cylinder and a three-quarter choke, or (if a special gun is to be purchased) a magnum fully choked in both barrels. It is certain with the latter that an occasional shot at seventy yards with No. 4 shot will come off, and there is something distinctly pleasing about the idea. It is almost equally certain that the standard load used with the standard gun presents an unjustifiable chance at this range. A compromise, of course, would be a second pair of barrels fully choked for the lighter gun—though not chambered for three-inch ammunition. The gas pressure of the big cartridge might be dangerously high, and it would be wiser to be content with the full choke.

For snipe-shooting the considerations are altogether different. Speed of shooting ranks equally with the importance of a close pattern. As there is no chance whatever of obtaining the latter at long range, a heavy gun is a disadvantage. This perhaps is another reason for keeping to a standard weapon if only one gun is to be purchased. The right type of ammunition for snipe is probably a standard cartridge filled with No. 8 shot.

It was suggested earlier that a pattern of 290 pellets is necessary to make sure of a kill, and such a pattern is satisfactorily provided by a half-choke up to forty yards. The improved cylinder at the same range should put 240 pellets into the circle, so one can reasonably say that it is fully efficient up to thirty-five yards. At the greater range, the energy retained by this pellet is actually less than the accepted minimum of ·8 foot-pounds. But the lighter build of a small bird such as a snipe almost certainly makes it vulnerable to the ·5 foot-pounds retained at forty yards. In this connection, one might suggest that the tough hide of a goose requires more penetration than the standard, while small birds will almost invariably succumb to something less.

The only other point for consideration is the length of the barrels. There have been many schools of thought on this subject and probably more inaccurate surmise than the facts warrant. For the past seventy years shooting men have sworn by guns whose barrels varied in length between 25 and 32 inches, and, generally speaking, they have all been right. Tests show that the loss in velocity for a short barrel is so

slight as to make little difference at sporting ranges.
The 25-inch barrel will kill almost as well and as far
as a 32-inch barrel if the standard ammunition is used.
The old fallacy that a gun with short barrels ought to
be lighter is exploded by the universally accepted
principle that weight must be governed by the charge
of shot.   It is consequently found that the manufacturers who supply guns with short barrels do not
necessarily make them any lighter.

At the same time, the wildfowler is likely to prefer
a 28-inch gun, in that there may be occasions when he
wishes to use a high-velocity cartridge.   Although
these only give an extra range of three or four yards,
the cartridge will have been presumably selected for
just this slight gain.   An H.V. loading is partially
wasted in a short gun, through the full expansion of
the gases failing to be completed by the time they
reach the muzzle.   For the same reason, a long cartridge
loses some of its advantages, and it is therefore seldom
that one comes across such a weapon with three-inch
chambers.

The points which I have set out in the preceding
paragraphs are those which a number of seasons after
duck and geese caused me to seek out.   They seemed
to provide the reasons for many missed shots, and as
such were personally satisfactory.   It would be pre-
sumptuous to suggest that they can be used as a guide
to shot-gun ballistics—a wide subject which has a
literature of its own.

CHAPTER V

MORE ABOUT GUNS

ONE day an easterly wind came screaming over the sea. I remember it not only for the spouting columns of white water which leapt up the face of the Red Head, but for the anxious moments of which it was the source. The first belonged to the morning as I was peering through the windscreen of my aircraft looking for the white line of foam which should have marked the land. I was one hour and fourteen minutes late on my estimated time of arrival at the coast, and the last fourteen minutes with only a few gallons of petrol swilling about in the bottom of the tank were unpleasant. I had hoped after that to make better use of the gale, for the flax pond on the cliff-top had been flooded by the recent October rains and I had seen the duck in the bays up the coast during the previous week. The combination was promising.

And so it turned out. But I had reckoned without my companion. When we unshipped ourselves and our baggage beneath the waving canopy of the wind-tortured trees of a near-by spinney, I noticed the gun. As soon as I saw it, I felt that the anxieties of the day were not done. It hung on a piece of cod-line tied between the trigger guard and the end of the single stubby barrel—a neglected fowling-piece with the aspect of one of those iron cannons used in the days of the Armada.

" I've just bought it," said my companion proudly, as he picked at the knot of the string.

It was too late to make fresh arrangements, for the dusk was already gathering about the cliffs, and it was time to strike across the fields from the trees where we had left the motor-cycle. The duck would be in early to-night.

I blamed the gale and the exceptional conditions which it had brought. The fact that I had been hoping for such a night had nothing to do with it, and I took it ill that the flax pond should have been the scene of this, my companion's first attempt at duck-shooting. I should be sharing a hide which would bring me within two feet of his cannon at the moment it went off. If there hadn't been a gale we should have gone to the little loch in the hills, where we would have been widely separated.

" How much did you pay for it ? " I asked, in a voice I tried to keep normal.

" Five shillings," he said, and then added : " I reckon it's worth a fiver any day, don't you ? "

But worse was to come. When we had crept into the little hide in which we sat shoulder to shoulder, with the muzzles of our guns poking through the matted branches, he produced a cartridge from a receptacle in his clothing which he assured me had a special high-velocity load. Never before had I hoped —no, prayed—that the duck would not come this way this night. The cartridge, I reckoned, would create a pressure of something like three-and-a-half tons to the square inch in the barrel. What would happen then I didn't care to guess—and probably should never know.

The weapon had come out of Belgium, perhaps with a returning soldier of the 1914 war. It was one of the cheaper products of a cheap country, and though its barrel looked massive enough, there was no substance to the face of the action. As if this wasn't enough, there was sufficient play to make a clicking noise between the barrel and the rest of the gun when it was waggled.

I was still ruminating on the chances of fate when

there was a whir of wings overhead, to be followed almost immediately by an explosion in my ear. Out of the corner of one eye I saw a curl of smoke drifting up from the leaky breech, and beyond it the animated face of my companion staring out into the water on his side of the pond. I heard the story a moment later. A flight of mallard had hurtled in from the south-east to make a sudden banking turn to land with a splash on the water fifteen yards away. There had been five of them, and John described how he had pulled the trigger as they had touched the water.

"By God, you should have seen the shot," he said. "It churned up the whole place."

In witness of it, two birds were even now lying on the pond, one of them flapping feebly. The spread of shot had been more than adequate. Driven by a high-velocity load up the stumpy barrel, twenty-four inches long, it had blasted the pellets like a charge of grape, to reap a harvest which even I conceded was satisfactory.

Once more that night the chance came for a shot, and then by the grace of Providence the night closed in, to make further shooting impossible. I am sure that the twilight has never given way to complete darkness so quickly. In less than half an hour we were isolated entities in a world of shrieking wind and inky blackness. By the light of a torch we collected four fine mallard before we groped our way across the fields to the hidden motor-cycle.

"That was pretty exciting," said my companion.

A few weeks later I stood beside my friend as he signed a cheque for fifty pounds. He had become an enthusiast for flighting, suddenly, like a man who is given a taste of the air in a sailplane and is restless and unhappy until he has mastered the art. But he was not going to practise the business with that gun while

The Findhorn. *See page* 61.

I was in the vicinity, and I had persuaded him in his own interests that the fifty pounds he was now signing away for a proper weapon was not only wise, but essential. If his life insurance company had heard of the Belgian gun, I believe that they would have paid the money for him.

I am, personally, an enthusiast for nice things. They appeal to me for their own sake and are a perpetual reminder, in an increasingly shoddy world, that craftsmanship has a value which is not to be expressed in ordinary terms. Some of us acquire such a view in early life, others need years to reach the same conclusions, and a few are content with makeshifts from the cradle to the grave. My education began with the possession of a little trout rod given me by my mother when I was a small boy. To-day, over thirty years later, the same rod is still my favourite. I have to thank my mother for something more than the rod itself, and the five-pound note which probably went to its purchase. It has been a lasting reminder that the highest class of tool lasts so well that it is the cheapest in the long run. In later years, a pair of Purdy guns which belonged to my father cemented the impression, and then these were followed by other things, leading finally to a 2000 horse-power Rolls Royce aero-engine behind which I flew for many hours, and whose superb workmanship was revealed periodically during its routine inspections.

Nothing, perhaps, hides its shortcomings so successfully as a cheap gun. It is only something really outstanding in the way of poor workmanship and materials which is immediately obvious. John's gun was a case in point. A more experienced sportsman would have known the risk he was taking and would have consigned the weapon to the rubbish-bin on the general grounds of humanity. But between this and the article for which a man pays 200 guineas there is a

F

Rough shoot. A fine mixture of cultivated land with plenty of cover and water to attract the duck.
See page 114.

range of weapons which look much the same and make one wonder whether the difference in price isn't to be found in the fineness of the engraving. A visit to Birmingham, where the best gun barrels in the world are made, and then to the workshops of any one of the dozen leading gunmakers, settles this question. In guns, like most other things, one gets what one pays for.

When I was looking for a new gun a few years ago I visited the showrooms of a London maker and handled a caseful of his products one after the other. I didn't inquire the price of any of them, but laid three aside whose handling qualities had made a special appeal. While I suspected that I was choosing something beyond my means, I didn't realise that I had picked out three of the highest grade guns which are made, each of them costing over £100. The interesting thing is that any shooter would have done the same thing, even if he was blindfolded. When I picked up a cheap grade of weapon immediately after handling the best grade, the difference was astonishing—though the weight of both guns was the same.

While a reputable maker will look after his customer to the extent of seeing that he gets the quality he is paying for, whether new or second-hand, it must be more satisfactory to know for oneself what is good and what is bad about a gun.

The qualities which count can be put down in their order of importance. It is for these that the discerning buyer will look.

1. An even distribution of shot over the area of pattern, without which there will be no guarantee that an accurate aim will be justly rewarded.
2. A long life—which is a quality derived from excellence of materials and workmanship.

3. A balance with the weight well between the hands
—a quality bound up with the basic design,
workmanship and materials.
4. A good fit.

It might be imagined that a medium-grade gun
would attain at least the first and most important of
these qualities. I don't believe, however, that this is
always true. It is possible to pay £50 for a serviceable-
looking weapon and to discover after testing it that its
pattern consists of clumps of pellets with correspond-
ing gaps, or more often a diffusion of pattern associated
with the blast effect of a high-velocity cartridge in a
true cylinder. It is then too late to discover that the
price paid for the highest grade of gun includes tests
for quality of pattern while the gun is still under con-
struction—irregularities being adjusted by a man who
works to thousands of an inch and to a standard which
only true craftsmen achieve. The identical machining
of two barrels, even to fine limits, does not guarantee
that they will shoot in the same way. It is perhaps
strange that in an enlightened world, governed largely
by exact science, a shot-gun barrel remains more or
less unpredictable until tests have proved it.

On the other hand, the only practical way of keeping the shot together at long ranges has been found to
constrict the last inch or two of the barrel up to a
maximum extent of forty-thousandth of an inch for a
full choke. This is a drastic impediment to the passing
shot, which even a lay mind can appreciate as a source
of pattern irregularities. If one imagines a column of
pellets travelling at 900 miles an hour coming suddenly
into a bottleneck, the ensuing confusion—although
lasting for an infinitesimal part of a second—is under-
standable. Looked at like this, it is less of a wonder
why shot-gun ballistics as they relate to patterns is not
an exact science. Even when an expert has made a

minute alteration to the contours of the bottleneck
(which experience teaches him will correct some particular fault in a pattern) a different load of shot, or
even another cartridge of exactly the same load, will
not give an identical pattern. It will only ensure the
desired density of shot to a characteristic pattern.

I have seen the rough ingot of carbon steel as it
comes from the founder's mould, and watched it as it
has passed glowing through the rolling mills to become
a flaky black bar to be roughly cut and bored. I have
seen the tube as it is delivered to the gunmaker, and
watched the almost incredible number of things which
are done to it before it emerges as a finished barrel.
At any moment a slight alteration to a procedure can,
and does, make the difference between something which
is fit for a top-grade gun and something only fit for a
much cheaper weapon.

Something of the history of a pair of barrels can be
read by anyone through an inspection of the breech.
If this is wiped clean, the way in which the two barrels
have been joined together is revealed by the line of the
brazing. If this is seen to be of the simple pattern
shown in Fig. 1,* it is a reasonable assurance that the
barrels are of the highest quality. It means that the
original tubes were supplied to the gunmaker with the
" lumps " forming an integral part of the barrel. The
subsequent machining has resulted in two perfectly
flat faces which are brazed together to form the strongest
possible joint for the lightest possible weight of metal.
In each of the three other methods illustrated (Figs. 2,
3, and 4)* the "lumps" are brazed on afterwards, not
merely adding to the final weight, but tending towards
clumsiness through the need of a brazing surface of
wide area. This is not to assert that any one of the
other methods are inefficient or dangerous. The great
majority of guns employ one or other of them. But
the cleaner design of Fig. 1 is to be found in a top-

* Pages 207 and 208.

grade gun, and it is a significant fact that the tubes from which they were made cost sixteen times as much as those on which the " lumps " did not form an integral part.

Unfortunately, an inspection of the breech such as I have described does not lead to the detection of anything which need prevent purchase. It will merely show whether the gun is top-grade or something else. It is in the case of a third or fourth grade weapon where a risk is run in regard to the safety of the barrels. In a cheap gun, particularly of foreign make, the quality of the steel ingot from which the tubes were originally bored may be inferior to the extent of secreting flaws. In all cases the steel used is what is known as " fluid compressed steel." That is to say, it is compressed hydraulically during the process of cooling after being poured into the mould. In spite of this, the core of the ingot, which solidifies last, will, owing to the contraction of the metal as it cools, contain pockets or flaws which should condemn it. While there is more than one method of checking this tendency of inferior metal towards the centre of the ingot, it is reasonably certain that its quality throughout is inconsistent, and usually the doubtful part is thrown away. At the same time, the old maxim that every penny counts, influences the production of the cheapest gun and it is possible that it may have been given a start which no amount of good workmanship can afterwards remedy.

But a perfect piece of steel can still be ruined during the process of manufacture, and particularly during the marriage of the two barrels by the brazing process. Great heat is required for this, and an inexperienced workman can easily apply too much. It is on cheap guns that the less expert craftsmen are set to work. The results are shown up under the microscope, and once seen they are not to be forgotten. The lovely close grain of the steel as it is seen at the breech (where the pressure of the discharge is the greatest) is now a coarse network of hairlines. Its power of resistance to pressure has been more than halved. At any point along the barrels the same disaster may have befallen, for the top and bottom rib is brazed from the breech to the muzzle.

At the same time, I don't think that the foregoing need be taken as anything more than a warning to the " Johns " of this world. We don't usually go to a back street in Brussels for our guns, and the makers over here who offer weapons for £25 or less still have a reputation which they value. Moreover, every British gun—whether the barrels are bored out of the solid bar, or " drawn " as is sometimes the case with the cheapest grades—still has to be proved. That is to say, they are officially submitted to a proof-house, where a special proving charge is fired and a pressure created in the barrels which leaves a substantial margin of safety.

The only other thing that need be said about barrels applies to those which are second-hand. The buyer will want to know the degree of choke in each bore, the amount of wear which has already taken place, and the extent of any imperfections. While any barrel which is choked must be so stamped, the degree is not usually marked. In the case of a new gun, this information is readily available. In the case of an old gun, the dealer will take the measurements for you with a proper instrument. Choke has already been mentioned many times in the preceding pages, but for convenience I give the complete table below :

Boring	Points of Choke (thousandths of an inch)	Percentage of Pellets in 30-inch circle at 40 yards
Full choke . . .	40	70
Three-quarter . .	30	65
Half	20	60
Quarter . . .	10	55
Improved cylinder	3–5	50
True cylinder . .	Nil	40

Wear in a barrel is detected by the same instrument as is used for measuring the choke. The standard internal diameter of a twelve-bore is ·729 inches, and although this will vary slightly from gun to gun, even in a new weapon, it should not normally be expected to approach the measurement of a thirteen-bore, which is ·710 inches. There have been numerous instances where a barrel has burst through the washing away of the metal caused by the scouring effect of the high-velocity gases and the passage of the shot. A barrel which is worn to " paper " thinness is obviously something to be avoided. This particularly applies to Damascus barrels, which weight for weight are less able to withstand high pressure. They are in any event likely to be of a mature age, for their manufacture was discontinued in favour of steel barrels (so far as the best guns are concerned) fifty years ago.

A secondary but equally important defect sometimes discovered in a cheap gun is a crooked barrel. It is possible that during the course of its manufacture it was given a curve. This is not a quality which makes for straight shooting, and it can usually be detected by holding it up to the light so that a shadow is cast in the form of a line from the muzzle to the breech. If this line is perfectly straight, however the barrel is revolved, the bore is straight. The same inspection will reveal a dent or hollow in the bore, for at this point the line of shadow will be interrupted. If the outer surface of the barrel is inspected, dents will be shown up as a dark blur.

A bore which is pitted is not necessarily unserviceable. If the pitting is only slight the barrel can be skimmed—that is to say, a minute quantity of metal can be taken away by the gunsmith to leave the bore slightly larger, but unblemished. This does not appear always to affect the shooting. I had the work done for a weapon of my own with satisfactory results. The alternative is to leave the barrel as it is, but to see that it is always cleaned and oiled with special care. The blemishes are particularly susceptible to rust.

The rest of the gun—the action, the locks, and the stock—will have been originally designed to match the barrels. That is to say, a fine pair of barrels is not normally fitted to an inferior action. For practical purposes, the matter of chief importance in a second-hand weapon, or even a new one, is the fit of the component parts. It is here that such infinite labour is expended in a top-grade gun that the selling price is materially increased. A new, but third-grade weapon, costing thirty pounds or more, may reveal many short-comings to the experienced eye even in the unused state. These are more patently demonstrated as the gun grows old. Not only do the movable parts become increasingly slack, but the weaker points of design are thrown into relief. The result is usually a breech which shows an appreciable gap between it and the face of the action. It is here that the backwards force of the explosion is exerted—and here where the various devices of anchorage leave most to be desired in design and workmanship.

The barrels of a gun are hinged at a point forward of the breech and below it. The hook on the forward " lump " is the connection. It is therefore obvious that any backwards pressure as the gun is fired has a tendency to open the gun. But there is more to it than this, for the steel of which the action casing is made has elastic qualities. These will allow it to spring under the shock of the explosion. It will therefore be seen that although there may be no visible gap between the breech and the face, the pressure of the explosion will momentarily create one unless the locking device is performing the function of a rigid anchorage. Lock-ing devices, whether of doll-neck or cross-bolt design —or both—often do nothing of the sort. Either a bad fit or a bad design, or sometimes a combination of the two, permits this fractional movement of the breech on firing. In the end it will lead to trouble.

More generally, the workmanship of the firing mechanism, regardless of the engraving, is an indication of the value of the gun. Accuracy of fit, which has originally entailed an enormous amount of hand-finishing, is an infallible yardstick. Whether the gun has the usual box lock—which is a basic design introduced in 1875 and is still the simplest and best—or a more modern side lock is a matter of little importance. If it is not intended to use the gun for other purposes than wildfowling, however, there are two final considerations which may make an inexpensive gun excellent value. The first concerns the ejector. Self-ejectors are not necessary when speed in reloading is of no importance. I suppose that the occasions when one has the opportunity of getting off four cartridges within a few seconds are rare. They certainly are in my own experience. As the self-ejector mechanism costs money, it can be saved. The second consideration is bound up with the same point. Some guns do not open as widely as others—very often because of a design which has paid special attention to the lock which keeps the gun closed and acts as the anchorage, of whose importance I have already written. This slows up the reloading process—and I suggest that the disadvantage can be accepted.

Yet when the problem is viewed as a whole, the only conclusion is that a top-grade weapon is worth the money. One may wonder why mechanical processes have not been introduced to take the place of the enormous amount of hand-fitting, remembering that many articles in common use are made to fine limits by machines alone. I can't answer my own question, for in this amazing age of mechanical genius I find it hard to accept the excuse that a shot-gun is not like other things which have yielded to and benefited from the machine.

The choice of a cartridge deserves the same consideration as the choice of a gun. I have several friends who, through some mistaken idea of economy, always buy the cheapest. After the toil of a long chase after wildfowl, the consummation of one's efforts ought to be given the best chance. Cheap cartridges don't always provide it. They are no more reliable than the curate's egg. But, worse—I have seen an experienced wildfowler dry out his cartridges after a wet outing, and then select the same ammunition for his next expedition. It is not so much a matter of whether a swollen case will go into the breech, but whether the turnover at the end of cartridge is still going to provide the same resistance to the expanding gases. A force of forty-five pounds is normally required before the turnover gives way and allows the shot to pass down the barrel. If it is less than this, the gas pressure will not build up to its designed maximum, and the velocity of the shot will suffer. At the extreme ranges so often used in wildfowling such a loss is fatal.

I would not wittingly risk a cartridge of which I had any doubts about the turnover, any more than I should employ an inferior gut cast for a salmon. On the other hand, it is probably unnecessary to pay the top prices asked for the highest grade of ammunition. The standard article sold by reputable manufacturers has been found to be consistent, and it is consistency for which the sportsman seeks. The extra money usually goes into special waterproofing of the case, and therefore only pays its dividend under extreme conditions. As a wildfowler, I have seldom had to swim, and the number of cartridges which have had to be discarded through getting wet are few. Perhaps it is largely because I am not a man who takes out twenty-five cartridges when half a dozen shots are the most to be expected. The handful which go with me find a warm and dry billet in a vest-pocket. It is only a leather cartridge bag exposed to a day of driving rain which accounts for appreciable losses, and under these conditions the specially waterproofed ammunition is probably worth the extra cost.

On the other hand, I will have nothing to do with the cheap cartridges advertised as being suitable for rabbits and the use of keepers. Independent tests have shown inconsistency in some of the most important respects, and a cartridge which cannot be relied upon is dear at any price. As for giving such cartridges to a keeper, the practice is to be deplored. He is the one man who is likely by his skill and his attention to duty to come within range of the proprietor's enemies. When a hoodie crow, or a stoat, or any dangerous vermin is on the end of the keeper's gun, it is false economy to give him a cartridge which may let the beast escape.

I am driven back on the memory of many a plea made by my friends when we have been talking of the high costs of sport. It is always couched in the same terms—" My dear chap, I can't afford it." Sometimes the subject is the lease of a rough shoot, sometimes the price of a gun, sometimes the wages of a keeper. I have found it difficult to be patient, for all I have been told is that my friend has never succeeded in making up his mind as to what he wants most in life. It is rare for us mortals to be in a position to obtain everything we want, and a process of selection is the obvious solution. One man tells me that he couldn't possibly afford a gun costing a hundred pounds. Yet his enormous car accounts for more than this in petrol and tax every year. It does not require a mathematician to compute how long it would take him to save up for the gun if he halved the horse-power of his vehicle. The fact that he does not care to do so is no concern of mine. But I fail to find any sympathy for him when he turns up at a shoot with an inferior weapon and believes (quite erroneously) that it accounts for his poor performance. I have already said that I happen to like nice things, a common enough trait, and one which I have tried to adapt to my means. It has meant the employment of inexpensive, and therefore inferior, articles in many sides of my life. But they are sides which I personally do not greatly care about. The saving has made it possible to be more extravagant in other directions—in my equipment for shooting and fishing, for instance. It involves an attitude of mind which has much to recommend it to the man who intends to buy a gun, rent a shoot, or do any of those things which form the subject of these chapters.

CHAPTER VI

SHOOTING STRAIGHT

IN brilliant sunshine, ten thousand feet above the Cornish peninsula, I had a series of lessons in shooting which unexpectedly improved my performance with a shot-gun more than anything else I can recall. It was, perhaps, curious that two aircraft travelling at some four miles a minute through these remote airy spaces should have an influence upon the fate of creatures which darted down the hedgerows, skimmed the marshes, or barely topped the highest trees.

Since I was given my first gun as a boy, I have often wondered why I should be such an indifferent shot, and have sometimes evolved a fresh theory to produce a temporary improvement. Had I attended a shooting school, to shatter a few score of clay-pigeons under expert tuition, there might have been less to discover under the auspices of this other school—expressly designed for the extermination of bigger game. But as my sporting education was neglected it remained for me to discover accidentally some of the principles I should have learned long before.

We travelled to ten thousand feet in two Seafires, wing-tip to wing-tip through a layer of stratus cloud. On breaking out into the sunshine on the upper side the glass of the bullet-proof windscreen was frosted, and the blinding light came into the cockpit in diffused rays. But soon the dry air and the sun cleared the frost, and we climbed on upwards across a field of snow-white cloud stretching from horizon to horizon. It was exciting and exhilarating, as it always is after leaving the gloomy and cloud-bound earth and then driving on through the overcast into the dazzling purity of the upper air.

The orders were simple. As members of an advanced combat school we were to practise the first exercise of a course designed to create fighter pilots. That the course was as well adapted to the requirements of an amateur wildfowler was no concern of the instructors, but it was a point which appealed to me before we had been in the air for an hour.

The initial business of the day was to follow the target aircraft and to open fire with a camera-gun from two hundred and fifty yards. A two-second burst was to be followed by a breakaway and a renewed attack from astern, and so on until the film was exposed. The object was to fix in the pilot's mind an unforgettable picture of how big an opposing fighter looks at exactly two hundred and fifty yards. There was nothing difficult about it, for the orange bars on the sight screen were set so that it was only necessary to overtake the target until its wing-span filled the gap between them. By the time this had been repeated on a score of occasions the dullest mind had imprinted upon it the image of his enemy at the standard range. Thereafter the range bars on the sight could be switched off (they were an electrical device) and the pilot could still place himself to within a few yards of the critical distance without their help. In due course, the exercise was repeated with larger aircraft acting as the target, so that finally one could place oneself at two hundred and fifty yards from any other object in the sky.

The connection between this exercise and the shot which is fired from a bog-hole at flighting duck, or at a partridge as it rises from a field, is less obscure than it might seem. Any sportsman who consistently misses his birds must have appreciated the point had he shared the cockpit of the Seafire with me that day. He would soon have been saying to himself, " I'm worse than I thought at judging distances."

If the target aircraft is translated into a game bird

the connection is obvious. Instead of accepting two hundred and fifty yards as the standard range, substitute thirty yards, and ask yourself whether you could pull the trigger of a shot-gun at this distance, whatever the size of the bird, its speed, angle, and conditions of light. Thirty yards is, of course, an arbitrary figure. But it is a fair standard for a twelve-bore, and a convenient distance by which other ranges may be assessed.

I have laboured the point because the hours spent above the clouds over Cornwall, to say nothing of those after game on the ground, have convinced me that the average person has only the vaguest idea of distances. It is recognised at all fighter schools that it is useless to teach a pilot the art of shooting until his estimation of range is automatic. It is probably equally true for the sportsman at ground-level, and I think that failure to recognise it leads to countless shots being fired out of range. At organised shoots, where birds are driven over the guns, there can be such a profusion of targets that one takes the nearer birds well within shot. The man in the next butt or at the next stand is barely fifty yards away, so that to fire at the wider targets would be poaching. But walking up in a line, or out on a lonely expedition, there are fewer static points from which to judge distance, and the result is that shots are taken at fantastic ranges. This must be particularly true of birds going away over a large and level field, or a moor, and of duck and geese at last light. In the first case there is no focus point, and in the second the shadow forms of wildfowl against the darkening sky are deceptive. It is now that a lucky pellet which kills outside the genuine range of the gun convinces the sportsman that his previous failures have been due to his inability to shoot straight.

At thirty yards a pigeon presents a picture to the eye of a certain size, while a pheasant and a snipe are something different. How many men even in a good

light can place each bird unerringly correct for range ?
When the problem is complicated by presentation at
different angles—overhead, at eye-level, head-on, and
abeam—then estimation of range for every variety of
game is difficult. Only by forming the habit of consciously measuring distances with the eye, and trying
to shoot at a predetermined range, can a start be made
towards building up a background by which future
estimation is instantaneous and instinctive.

The fighter course revealed other parallels. Each
day the journey was made through the cloud sheet
(an anti-cyclone with a static inversion was covering the
British isles) and up into the sunshine, where new
lessons were learnt. We would go up in close formation
at a hundred and sixty miles an hour, my eyes glued
to the instruments and the eyes of the other pilot glued
to my aircraft. Had we drifted apart we should have
been invisible to each other at twenty yards. Then
once in the clear we arranged the exercise on the radio
telephone, and my companion acting as target would
go into a steady turn, describing a circle perhaps a mile
in diameter. The stage for the next lesson was set—
the lesson of estimating the line of flight, which has the
closest parallel to the swing of a shot-gun from the
moment it is raised to pulling the trigger.

As the attacker, I flew a circle inside my target, and
therefore made a tighter turn. I had to imagine a line
drawn ahead from the nose of the target in a curve
representing his line of flight. I then put my sights
on to his cockpit and pulled my aircraft ahead down his
projected track. To do this it was only necessary to
tighten my circle and, provided I did it accurately, the
target slid backwards across the sight screen, with its
nose pointing ever towards its centre.

During this process the fire-button was pressed
and the range kept constant at two hundred and fifty
yards. It was extraordinary how difficult it was—even

The Den. *See page* 114.

This flooded ground usually produced a duck or two.   *See page* 114.

If a gun stood where the white arrows are marked, the pigeons would run a
shuttle service.   *See page* 143.

to quite experienced pilots—to correlate each of the simple requirements. The films were analysed every day and projected on to a screen so that it was possible to see where the bullets would have gone. We were greatly impressed by how wide a miss was the result of a small error, and I know that many pilots felt that their chances of shooting down an enemy seemed remote. Yet constant practice showed a rising graph of hits, and slowly but surely one acquired confidence. Nothing could be truer for the sportsman who tries to improve his own shooting by practice, and persuades himself of the importance of such trifles as the swing of his gun down the line of flight. While this is a point which may be subconsciously realised by most shooters, it is probably left too much to instinct and too little to intellect. It was the analysis of the combat films which demonstrated that a hit made under any other conditions was a fluke. It equally showed that it was impossible to miss if the conditions had been satisfied and the correct deflection had been applied. I thought of all the partridges I had missed after they had got up in front of me. Had I persistently overlooked their rising line of flight, to shoot below them, just as I had shot behind the high birds which were going away and were on a descending line of flight ? There was nothing new in these discoveries, but it was novel to stumble across them two miles high.

The third and last series of lessons was comparatively simple—although it might be less easy to apply when standing in a turnip-field. From an aeroplane, deflection shooting is a matter of mechanics. On the ground with a shot-gun it is an instinctive process inspired by experience.

Sitting forward against the pull of the harness, and looking out through the armoured glass at an enemy rapidly growing in size, one sweeps in on a quarter attack with an ever-narrowing angle between the two

G

aircraft, and assessing this angle with an accuracy born of experience the attacker uses the mechanics of the sight to put on the required deflection. He doesn't guess that he must fire twenty or thirty yards ahead if he is to hit the enemy. He places him in the precise position within the ring of the sight to know that he can't miss. His lessons have taught him that, for every angle which is created between the two aircraft by the curve of pursuit, there is a specific position in the gun-sight which the target must be made to occupy. The attacker knows these positions by heart.

If the fighter is fitted with the latest gyroscopic sight, even this is looked after on his behalf, and it is only necessary for him to get the enemy into the sight before pressing the fire-button. The gyroscopes in the instrument put on the deflection.

But if I have made the destruction of an enemy appear easy, I should add a word of warning—one which applies also to the sportsman on the ground. Only an enemy who fails to see his attacker continues sedately on his original course, and only then is he " cold meat " under the guns of a good shot. His position under these conditions is as precarious as that of a driven pheasant, one of the few sporting birds which makes little attempt to take avoiding action. The man who realises that he is being attacked ought to be as unpredictable as a snipe, and it is only the most intelligent anticipation which enables the attacker to estimate his enemy's flight path during the vital seconds when he is within range. And because two men fighting each other in the air are highly trained and quick-thinking individualists, a victory in combat represents skill on a high plane.

The bird which comes under fire doesn't know his attacker's weaknesses—whether he is worse at a crossing target or one which is climbing. It doesn't know the size of shot which is being used and, consequently, the dangerous range. But two well-matched human adversaries know a tremendous amount about each other. They know, for instance, which aircraft is faster in a dive or a climb—vital knowledge if one of them is trying to escape. They know that aerobatics are useless as a means of escape, but that a turn made tighter than the attacker's is a certain shield. Their speed and manœuvrability at every height and in every position are known to each other, and a score of decisions must be made correctly before one of them is in a position to press the fire-button.

It is perhaps fortunate that air tactics do not enter into a sportsman's education, and maybe lucky that the necessity to shoot in inverted attitudes is rarely necessary ! As an example of the latter, an exercise known as " the upward twizzle " helps to maintain respect between the exponents of the two arts. This attack consists of a steep dive from about two thousand feet above the enemy, and continues to a point about two thousand feet below him. From here the attacker pulls up into a more or less vertical climb at a very high speed, and if black-out hasn't already ruined the attack, an aileron turn, succeeded by the first half of a barrel roll, brings the aircraft into the necessary curve of vertical pursuit. Then when the range closes to two hundred and fifty yards the button is pressed with the required deflection and the barrel roll completed for the breakaway. No bird I have ever met on the ground has demanded comparable contortions.

On the other hand, the sportsman probably has a greater range of speeds to assess, and, most certainly, many more angles. With the pre-gyro gun-sight a greater " angle off " than thirty degrees was impracticable (if there was to be any certainty of success), whereas the man with the shot-gun can meet in a day's shooting with every angle in a three-dimensional sphere. Moreover, the speed of an enemy can be assessed by the experienced fighter pilot, for although both may be travelling at five miles a minute it is the relative speed between them which slows the process down to manageable proportions.

A rabbit bolted from its burrow possibly travels at fifteen miles an hour over average ground, and considerably less if it is really rough. A grouse driven downwind may be moving at seventy miles an hour. One is about five times as fast as the other, and the deflection problem without mechanical aids is not an easy one. I was once shooting pigeons above a clearing in a wood of high trees and had fired twelve cartridges without bringing down a bird. It was a wide clearing, and there was plenty of time to assess the range, to judge the line of flight, and to pull the barrels of the gun along their projected path. There was no reason why the birds shouldn't have been tumbling down. The conclusion was that I was hopelessly misjudging the correct deflection—a fault due to either an inaccurate assessment of the range or the speed of the targets, or perhaps both. Looking back afterwards, I was certain that my estimate of the range was wrong. At any rate, I consciously began to swing the gun far past the point at which instinct told me to pull the trigger, and immediately the pigeons began to make that brilliant aerial wriggle which denotes that the pellets have passed just in front of their beaks. The next move was the last one, for it was only necessary to reduce the deflection by a trifle. I fired eleven more cartridges and killed ten birds.

Unfortunately, in a day's rough shooting, when every new target may be travelling at a different speed and in a different direction, there is no opportunity for experiment. It is now that experience intelligently applied comes to the rescue. If one is determined enough to give it a chance—that is, to resist the temptation to pull the trigger at any other ranges than those

one knows—then the right deflection will be instinctively
applied and a disastrous start may be followed by a
brilliant recovery. But this will be impossible if the
first lessons have not been learnt. It can only be true
when the assessment of range is sound and the line of
flight has been faithfully projected. The mechanics
by which these ends may be reached are simplified by
an understanding of the velocities which are involved.
But before discussing these there are still a few more
elementary factors which should be introduced.

I have had the chance of watching many good shots
in the field and every one of them has a quality which
can best be called " style." It is a quality to be noticed
elsewhere—on the football field, the golf course, and
in a squash racquets court. To have seen Hughie
Gallacher shoot the winning goal at a football match,
or Amr Bey polish off his opponent in the squash
court, or Henry Cotton drive a golf ball, is to understand
the underlying meaning of the word. It is a composite
thing, like a cocktail, and the ingredients include
rhythm, balance and timing. I saw Jackie Brown win
the World's Flyweight Boxing Championship, and
during this, his heyday, he piled on a hurricane of blows
which led to the boxing writers making guesses about
the number of blows he struck in a single second. He
proved that speed and timing were not incompatible.
Watching him, one could see that his secret was his
wonderful footwork, and, of course, this provided the
balance which was so vital. Amr Bey in his own sphere
relied on the same thing, and every photograph which
has been taken of him in action shows a balanced body.
Henry Cotton has the same quality in a more static
form. If you watch him pick up a ball from an awkward
hanging lie you cannot help noticing how firmly planted
are his feet, how well the balance is preserved as he
swings.

The first-class shot has many of the qualities of

these stylists. Basically, the foundation of his success is his footwork. The point can be demonstrated with a camera during a day's rough shooting anywhere. A photographer walking up with a line of guns across a field of roots has all the raw material required. The man at the end of the line who is missing his birds consistently appears in a damning light when the film is developed. He is seen to be firing with one foot off the ground, with his body twisted at unnatural angles, and even in positions from which one would conclude that he was about to fall over. But the next man, a first-class shot, appears perfectly poised as he pulls the trigger. At a casual glance, one might suppose that he had been lucky—that the birds had got up when his feet were firmly planted on the crests of the furrows. But such a conclusion would be unfair, for either by instinct or practice he has developed his footwork so that even on the roughest ground he succeeds in establishing a poise which makes a free and rhythmic swing a certainty.

On level ground the difficulties are obviously less. But even here I have seen snapshots of men in ugly positions. Therein lies one reason for mediocre per- formances—a suggestion which in no way denies the precepts put forward earlier, but makes their application an impossibility. It is, moreover, an explanation why a man may be good at driven birds—where his stand is prepared—but poor under other conditions.

Many tantalising recollections remind me of how impossible I have made conditions for myself through a bad stance. One day I was shooting partridges when we came to a large field of roots bordered on one side by an escarpment. There were a dozen guns out, and half of them were to go round to the other side and bring the birds towards the remainder waiting along the line of high ground. I was to be one of those who stayed behind, and in choosing my stance I selected a place on the slope. At first sight it looked a good place. If I stayed below the birds would be at least fifty feet up, and as they would be travelling on a stiff breeze they would be extremely difficult. The instinct was to reduce the distance between the gun and the game. The top of the rise was impossible, for not only would it mean shooting down into the advancing line of " beaters," but it was so irregular that anything like a line of guns would have been impossible. So the middle part of the slope, where it was not so steep and where the feet could get a fair grip, appeared to be the obvious place. Nor was I the only one to choose a similar stance.

There were nine or ten coveys in the field—perhaps sixty birds altogether—and they came over in a way that shooters dream about—high and fast and straight. There were always a few yards between each bird, so that the chance of getting the first one out of a bunch of five and then taking the last in the same group was never better. Yet until the end of the drive I never hit a bird. It wasn't the partridges which had the better of me, but the slope.

There was only one position in which I was comfortable, and of course I never had a chance at just that angle. I was making awkward twists and turns, unable to keep steady on my feet, unable to make a smooth swing without overbalancing. One foot would slip at the last moment, and as soon as the position had been retrieved the next chance would be upon me, but from a new angle which overbalanced me once again. As I say, I shot nothing until the end of the drive, and only then after I had moved to the bottom of the escarpment. From here I killed clean a brace which streamed fast and high overhead, restoring a little of my confidence.

There are said to be men who can shoot from any position. I certainly know of one fighter pilot who is as accurate in an inverted turn as he is on the level, and

I have seen a man hit a ping-pong ball with a revolver
after it has been thrown into the air. It is best not to
disbelieve anything in the shooting world. But the
ordinary mortal asks for a stance which gives him a
chance of making a free swing, leaving him at the end
of it as firmly planted on his feet as he was at the
beginning.

There was a " skeet " range on a piece of waste
ground close to the headquarters of the combat school
and pilots were encouraged to put some of the theories
they had learnt in the air into practice on the ground.
No one was sure whether it could contribute to some
future air victory, and I myself was firmly convinced
that it could do more harm than good to a man's game-
shooting. But there was no doubt about its value in
reminding one of the importance of the line of flight,
and it helped also to develop an easy swing of the gun.
Unfortunately a " skeet " has a flight which is on a curve
of de-acceleration while nearly all game, except driven
game, is accelerating. The partridge which gets up
as the guns advance probably does not reach its peak
speed for ten yards, and it starts from scratch. Some
game, such as snipe, are quicker off the mark than
others. But everything which is flushed must increase
its speed progressively. Apart from this disadvantage,
the " skeets " had a constant flight path and never varied
in their speed. One knew exactly what to expect, with
the result that most of us became so deadly that it was
easy to believe that the problems of game-shooting had
been satisfactorily solved. I frequently saw a pilot
go round the six stands, firing six shots at each stand,
to " kill " thirty-five out of the thirty-six discs.

Of course, at an orthodox shooting school the
traps are set with more cunning, so that the " birds "
come to the shooter over the tops of trees and not
always from the same direction. Or they are released
from a tower to simulate high pheasants, or from a

hollow to suggest driven grouse over rising ground. But even here it is probable that more is learnt as a result of the instructor watching his pupil. It is he who intervenes with the remark that the head is being lifted, or that the butt of the gun is finding a different seating on the shoulder at each shot. One is inclined to take things like these so much for granted that a visit to a school will do more good than any casual practice at the traps. Such faults as a variable resting-place for the butt are more common than is imagined, and the cure is not always an alteration to the fitting of the gun. A good shot will continue to shoot well if he is given a weapon which doesn't fit him, just as an expert like Henry Cotton will hit a ball two hundred and fifty yards off the tee with any driver in the clubmaker's shop. If the gun fits well enough, it is doubtless more important to do a daily dozen swings every morning—a practice which will eventually fit the butt into the shoulder in any attitude of the body. Personally, I don't do this, preferring to enjoy my fair share of misses with my friends.

The " skeets " were easy for another reason. I was always ready. They did, however, serve to remind me how unready one often is in the field. The time which elapses between seeing game rise and firing the gun is long enough to jeopardise the chances without pro-longing it unnecessarily. By timing a companion with a stop-watch, it seemed that one and three-fifth seconds could easily elapse between first seeing the target and pulling the trigger. In this period a bird which is going away and averaging twenty miles an hour opens the range by another sixteen yards. If it gets up at twenty-five yards, it is therefore forty-one yards away before the shot leaves the barrel. When it is realised that teal in full flight are perhaps travelling thirty yards every second, geese, wild duck and grouse up to twenty-five yards a second, pheasants twenty yards, and partridges only a little less, then it is obvious that the man who is quick with his gun enjoys a tremendous advantage.

I once timed a party of guns under the varying conditions of a day's rough shooting. One individual who carried his gun over his shoulder took as long as three seconds before he fired, and another who carried it in the crook of his arm required two seconds. One cannot afford such time-lags when the birds are being flushed. Late in the season, when game is getting up at not less than thirty yards, the slow man never has a chance. The experiment made me realise why I missed so much when my gun was carried over my shoulder, my pipe was in the wrong corner of my mouth, and my thoughts elsewhere !

Remembering the foregoing considerations, one can now examine briefly the special characteristics of a shot-gun and cartridge. I have already said something about their qualities—or the lack of them—in the last two chapters. It is sufficient, therefore, to recall only those characteristics which affect straight shooting. The factors which probably arise most often—at any rate in conversation with my friends—might be listed as follows :

1. The permissible error in aim at various ranges.
2. The allowances which ought to be made for a crossing bird.
3. The effect upon the pattern caused by swinging the gun.

The last in this list can best be dealt with first, for it offers the opportunity of disposing of a popular misconception. This is that a moving barrel has the effect of spraying the shot, and consequently of giving a greatly elongated pattern. This is untrue, and for practical purposes it can be said that movement of the gun has very little effect on the pattern. Many experiments have been made, and the results show that where a standard cartridge is loaded with No. 6 shot, the number of pellets found in a thirty-inch circle at forty yards is reduced from about 150 for a stationary target to 125 for a moving target—and this for an improved cylinder. In the case of a full choke the reduction is less—from 190 pellets to 180. While it is possible that this reduction might allow a small bird flying fast across the line of shot to escape, it is not a worthy subject for sleepless nights. It is the man who checks his swing at the moment of firing who will have regrets to nourish. Invariably he misses the target by a wide margin to the rear—a fault which is not due to the gun or the ammunition, but to the time-lag in his own physical reactions.

This is not meant to deny the stringing of a shot column, which becomes more accentuated as the range increases, and if a long cartridge is used proportionately greater. A shot-gun cartridge does string, so that there may be twelve feet between the first and last pellets of a column at forty yards. But what we are prone to overlook is that 50 per cent. of the entire charge is concentrated into less than four feet at forty yards, and 75 per cent. within five feet. It is only a small proportion of the pellets which lose their initial velocity so that they lag far behind, and these in any case have probably lost their killing power. At forty yards, for instance, the energy contained in the last pellet is only half that of the leading pellet, and while both remain lethal for No. 6 shot at this range, at fifty yards one-quarter of the entire shot column might be said to be ineffective. This does not alter the conclusion that at practical ranges the stringing of shot has no decisive influence upon pattern, and therefore accurate shooting. At the most, it is a limitation affecting extreme range.

The permissible error of aim, which appeared first in my list (merely because it forms the basis of a question most often asked), is linked with what I have

already written. Reduced to figures, it amounts to a
matter of twenty-two inches at forty yards with an
improved cylinder, and eighteen inches with a full
choke. The more significant point which arises is the
permissible error at close range. At twenty yards, for
instance, the shot has not had a chance to spread,
and therefore aim must be much more accurate.
The entire shot column is concentrated into a circle
of sixteen inches with a fully choked barrel and
about twenty-six inches in the case of an improved
cylinder.

In view of this, little more need be said of the
disadvantages of a full choke for ordinary game-
shooting.

We now come to the last of my points—the allowances to be made for crossing birds. First of all, the
popular belief that a high-velocity cartridge affects this
can be disposed of. The difference between an H.V.
and a standard load is a matter of a very few inches, and
for all practical shooting can be ignored. In the following table figures are shown for birds crossing at right
angles at speeds of forty and sixty miles an hour.
Higher speeds than this must be rare, and far more often
than not the birds are flying at something less than a
right angle to the shooter. The figures, however, will
provide some guide to the distances which are involved:

Range	40 m.p.h.	60 m.p.h.
20 yards	$3\frac{1}{2}$ feet	$5\frac{1}{2}$ feet
30 yards	$5\frac{3}{4}$ feet	$8\frac{3}{4}$ feet
40 yards	$8\frac{1}{2}$ feet	$12\frac{1}{2}$ feet
50 yards	$11\frac{1}{2}$ feet	$17\frac{1}{4}$ feet
60 yards	15 feet	22 feet

I have endeavoured in these pages to suggest some
of the factors which enter into straight shooting. There

are certain to be many sportsmen who have never considered them and yet shoot very well. But then there are men in other branches of sport who ignore the orthodox approach, and in writing what I have I do not want to convey any more than that I have found the foregoing considerations useful.

CHAPTER VII

OUR SHOOT

EVERY year when the corn is being cut I see around me the devastating efficiency of the race to which I belong. The sight of tidy fields, clipped hedges, clean ditches—in spite of the summer growth about them ; of drained bogs, felled coverts, and reclaimed heaths ; the sight of these things, and more besides, give me a despairing sense of righteous efficiency.

We have wrought indescribable good in an England which must once have been quite different. No doubt we are not individually to blame. But as I look on the mechanical reapers reaping the chemically boosted corn in the geometrical fields I feel that I should like to see it all abandoned—that the weeds should grow again, the scrub and the thickets spread over the downs, the valleys flood, and the oak and the beech come back into their own beside a few meadows. Unfortunately, inefficiency is a threat to the progress of a species which has decided that to multiply indefinitely is a divine task. Rabbits have the same instinct, but not the advantages. By the will of providence—or a flaw in the mathematics relating to averages—men have acquired all the trump cards, and we are using them to build up a tremendous score. The wild only lives by courtesy. There will come a time when we are so numerous that every animal which cannot be conceived, born, weaned, and fattened for the kill within a few weeks will become an un-economical liability. And we all know what will happen then : it will disappear. The last sentence is the clue to my pennyworth of philosophy. It is the vision in the crystal seen by sportsmen who are looking for that elusive, hard-to-define thing known as a " rough shoot."

I have tramped over many acres looking for over-grown ditches and similar signs of bad farming. In recent years they have been hard to find—or the agricultural committees have found them before me, and put in another farmer. The days when agriculture was not even fit for the younger sons of the peerage have gone. The peers themselves are lucky to possess farms to-day, and the immediate result is that the places where pheasants and partridges prefer to nest no longer exist, and the haunts of the snipe and the wild-fowl are producing food or grazing cattle. It has not meant, of course, the extinction of rough shooting. But it has involved a new approach to it and the necessity for being satisfied with less.

" I think," said a friend, one day, " I have found the place we are looking for."

He was a partner in an enterprise which we hoped would keep our larders interesting during the winter months. When he reeled off a list of the prospective game, which included pheasants, partridges, wild duck, snipe, grouse, hares, and rabbits, I could not hide my impatience to see it. His find smacked more of an estate of many thousands of acres than a modest area of inexpensive shooting to be covered in a day's walk.

But my partner was an unusual man, and his eye for the main chance was unrivalled. He was also an astonishing shot, although not always an orthodox one. On the first day we motored out to inspect our " property " he stopped the car suddenly at a side road, and pointing up the lane whispered " pheasant." He had hardly spoken when a rifle was in his hands and the door of the car was open. A moment later I heard a clatter of wings, and saw an old cock making off between the trees which bordered the lane. But it didn't get far, for my friend brought it down with his rifle as though it was a barnyard rooster on a perch. In less than a minute we were on our way again, and

my partner was talking animatedly of the country ahead,
apparently dismissing the incident as too trifling for
comment.

His skill, and his promptness in exploiting opportunity, were later to be reflected in our bags.

I think the ground over which we walked that
afternoon was the ideal of a large body of sportsmen
who think in the modest terms of a rough shoot. It
lay in a broad valley whose northern side rose to broken
crags and warm-tinted heather—the home of a few
coveys of grouse. In the groin of the valley was a
chain of lakes and a waste of scrub and marsh, which
not only spelled wild duck, but a sanctuary for the
pheasants which would be driven out of the coverts
and the fields or the cultivated slopes of the southern
side. It had that ideal combination of water, waste,
and efficient agriculture which is so rare. We became
the tenants, and were not disappointed.

It would be pleasant to write of the days which
we spent upon it, of the ways in which it was worked,
and of the floods followed by the frosts which brought
in the wild duck. But first I feel that a duty is owed to
all landlords by whose courtesy game is shot, and
perhaps to ourselves who have a respect for the land
and an affection for its creatures. It is easy enough
to take a shoot, to scour it as a woman might scour a
dirty pan, and to move on the following year to fresh
ground, leaving the old bare of game. But it is no
more decent to shoot out an area than it is to clear a
trout stream by netting. In the recent war I had
friends among our Allies who sometimes came out to
shoot or fish, and the attitude of some was not dis-
similar to a few members of our own community who
should know better. One asked why we didn't use
pump guns ; another had ideas for night lines, nets,
and explosives. It is true that a pump gun shooting
five cartridges might, in the hands of a first-class

The arrow shows the entrance to the passage
leading to the hole in the field. *See page* 138.

shot, account for five partridges out of a big covey. It is also true that a night line, or a net, or a bomb would double and treble the number of fish taken out of a river. By the same premises, the genius of science could no doubt dispose of every living creature in an entire county on a single afternoon. But what then? The living are dead, the earth bare, and in our mouths there must be a bitter taste. We need to remind ourselves sometimes that the instinct for efficiency which drives forward the chariot of progress does not pay a dividend in sport. I think that the ban placed on certain rivers upon upstream spinning for trout with a thread line—in spite of the skill required—is wise. It is the same kind of wisdom which decrees that it is "bad form" to use a pump gun.

Yet there may be some who, while agreeing, still do not appreciate the debt which, as good sportsmen, we owe to a rough shoot. The years of war ought to have reminded us, for great areas of sporting ground were without a keeper. Not a pheasant's egg was set; not a weasel, or a stoat, or a hawk, or a crow, or a hedgehog, or a rat was destroyed. The supply of game dwindled, and meanwhile the earth was cultivated intensively to the detriment of the rough places beloved by nesting birds. Unless a man has the honest intention of keeping down vermin, and promoting the well-being of the game, his moral rights to enjoy sport must be in question. A hundred years ago there was the strongest feeling on the matter. Industrialists and successful tradesmen from the towns were beginning to come out to the country and take up shooting rights alongside a sporting community with a rigid code. The keenest resentment was felt, not for reasons of snobbery, but because the countryman felt that the country was his own preserve, while the town remained the preserve of the townsman. That feeling has died. But if a preserve is leased by a townsman, he is expected

I have looked down upon the forest . . .
See page 144.

H

to recognise the rules and traditions by which sport
has flourished for hundreds of years.

Often a tenant's means are limited. But this does
not absolve him of his liabilities. He will remember
that his own neglect will have its repercussions on his
neighbours. If a keeper cannot be afforded, and he has
not the time to spend several days a week on the ground
himself, he may fall back on the help of the farmers or
their men, persuading them through friendship or
promise of reward, or both, to undertake some of the
necessary work.

If a schedule of the more essential duties of the
incoming tenant was to be drawn up, it would include,
in the first place, a complete reconnaissance of the
ground—which will enable him to assess the quantity
of game upon it and the extent to which it is the prey
of vermin. The earlier in the season such a reconnaissance is made the better, and if possible the shoot
should be taken over in February, before the nesting
season.

As soon as this has been done, one of the first
considerations must be the best means of increasing
the stock. If the shoot has been taken on a lease for a
number of years it is surprising how much enthusiasm
can be brought to the problem. One quickly discovers
that one has not so much bought up the rights to kill,
as the rights to nourish and multiply.

Every rough shoot with which I have had anything
to do has relied on partridges and wild pheasants as
its principal sources of sport. The features of the
ground which have attracted me are illustrated in some
of the photographs. On page 81 the waste of scrub
and thorn and bramble, with the flooded areas in the
low-lying parts, are the type of sanctuaries of which
I have spoken. Partridges and pheasants will always
use such cover, and if there are birds in the district
they will remain within reach of it. On page 96 is

another photograph which shows a den running down
to the sea. It has steep sides, overgrown with bramble
and gorse, and in its higher reaches trees line the sides.
This is another kind of sanctuary, and one which even
the most conscientious farmer is never likely to destroy.
This particular den has always produced sport.

I like bracken, too, on steep hill-sides facing south ;
and disused quarries which in high summer become a
riot of vegetation. Nor should the charms of a stream
be overlooked. Not only does it provide a source of
drinking water during a dry season, but its overgrown
banks are harbours for many kinds of game.

I remember one day walking over some prospective
ground with a friend and peering into a dark covert
of close-set pines. " We ought to be able to keep
pheasants here," he said.

But he was wrong—or partially wrong. On a rough
shoot, where the birds are likely to have to look after
themselves, I would sooner see an open wood of beech,
oak, birch, and pine, with a heavy undergrowth of
brambles and rhododendrons.

While pheasants roost in trees at night, they seem
to have a tremendous liking for the undergrowth
during the day, when they are not feeding in the
fields.

When there are plenty of sanctuaries such as these,
with perhaps the addition of one or two bridle-paths,
the nesting problems are less complicated by an efficient
farmer and his tractors. What then remains is to see
that, within the limits of human control, the eggs are
successfully hatched. It is in this duty that the keeper
shows his worth. I have often enough walked round
our ground with a gun, accounting here and there for
an occasional weasel, a stoat, a hawk, and less often a
hoodie crow. But I have never constructed a successful
tunnel trap, or done more than touch the serious problem
of vermin. Stoats and weasels kill for the love of killing,

and one's best chance of shooting them is that vital second when they sit up and listen, during their retreat. With small shot they are easy prey. But to find the holes in which they live and to bait them with a bitch of their own species, or to trap their runs, is only within the capabilities of the man who lives on the ground, and is prepared to learn the tricks of the trade. They are tricks which should be mastered without delay when rabbits are found with their necks eaten out, and game chicks with minute punctures on the sides of their heads. The latter will have a shrivelled appearance, and the indictment can be made out in the name of a weasel or a stoat.

We had a kestrel on our ground, and I used to see her in the spring pinned against the sky on motionless wings over the ridge where a few grouse were nesting. She chose the windward slope, where the up-currents were sufficient to support her weight and allow her to swing from point to point as each section of the rock and heather was examined by her keen eyes. Once, when I was lying on the sunny side of a grey boulder, I saw her coming towards me to take up a new station. She hung herself on the rising air almost overhead, just allowing me to keep out of sight behind the rock. It was obvious she had seen something, for within a few seconds I saw her give a curious little wriggle in the air, to be followed by a sensational stoop on half-closed wings. For perhaps a hundred feet she shot downwards, and I do not think that she applied her wonderful dive brakes until she was within ten feet of the ground. For a fraction of a second she was held in sudden check on braced wings before she disappeared gently into a clump of heather forty yards away. I covered the place with my gun, and when she rose again I fired and missed. I thought I saw something in her bright yellow claws— though I couldn't be sure—and she went rocketing down the hill-side towards the woods.

There had been no cry, no scream as you sometimes hear in the woods at night when a rabbit is caught unawares, and when I walked over to the place where the kestrel had stooped there was no sign of any living thing. Had she killed a grouse chick? If this had been the victim, then the remainder of the family and the parents were lying uncommonly well hidden. The episode was over, the moor empty again, and I sat down on a rock feeling particularly incompetent.

I have had more success in destroying the little brown sparrow-hawk. When one is lucky enough to see her and yet remain unseen, as she is watching an intended victim from the branch of a tree, a shot may be possible. The very method of her hunting occasionally lays her open to attack herself. Rigid, save for the movement of her eyes, she sits and waits, the embodiment of concentration, as her unconscious victim approaches. And then like a rocket projectile she launches herself into the attack. On a turn she must be one of the swiftest of all birds of prey.

It is not often that one sees a falcon, although once, on the high ground where a little oasis of water was sheltering a few wild duck, I saw an extraordinary commotion which almost resembled an aerial dog-fight, and which I think owed its origin to a falcon. I had been watching a flight of teal, which I first saw swinging in orderly formation over the water. I thought that I had put them up myself, although I had not seen them rise. Then into this came a thunderbolt which scattered the birds like chaff. Out of the confusion came two birds flying at extraordinary speed. The one in front was a teal, and the one behind a hawk. Where it had come from I had no idea, but for a few brief seconds I saw a chase at such a speed as flesh and feather can rarely attain. They passed me, apparently unmindful of my presence, although I was in full view, and disappeared over a little rise. The teal was leading by half a dozen yards, and if it maintained its speed it probably escaped.

One is bound to feel admiration for the hawks. If courage, skill, and vitality count for anything, the shooter's instinct is to withhold his fire. I remember wounding a hawk, and looking into its still defiant eyes —a blazing tawny-yellow—as I went to dispatch it. Such courage as I saw deserved a better fate. Yet among the feathered tribes few birds can do more damage, and, though they may be protected by law in some areas, the less often they are seen the better.

As opposed to hawks, there can be little sympathy for the carrion and hoodie crow. As egg-stealers they rank second to none (although some keepers will say that a jackdaw runs them close). It is not often that they give the casual shooter a chance of a shot, and most of those which are destroyed are the victims of wire-cage traps, or well-set egg traps. The manner of constructing them is no part of this book. But for those who are doubtful of the difference between a carrion and an ordinary rook, they need have few qualms about shooting if they see a rook-like bird hunting alone, or a " rook's " nest alone in a tree. A successful shot will produce a " rook " which has no bare patch round the base of its beak.

Rats, hedgehogs, jays, foxes, moorhens, and in parts of northern Scotland wild cats, are all on the list of criminals. The true wild cat is an untameable hunter, a master in the art of stalking, and is rarely seen by man. A friend who lives in the wilds of Ross found a litter a year or two ago and brought the kittens to his house, where he fed them by hand. Although he did everything possible to tame them, they remained balls of fury whenever he approached. He showed me photographs of the kittens—snarling atoms of venom which had the look of a cornered tiger. He never dared to put his hand into their cage. The best that can be

said about a wild cat is that its skin will make a remarkably fine pair of fur gloves. The tough hard fur from
its big body is the warmest I have ever worn.

But it is unnecessary to live in the far north to
suffer from cats, for the domestic farmyard variety can
develop a taste for hunting. They look innocent
enough by day, but when you see the gleam of their
eyes at night in the beam of a torch, or catch a glimpse
of a shadowy form at dusk as it slinks through long
grass, the potentialities are suggestive.

The suppression of vermin is possibly all that many
tenants of a rough shoot will be able to do in the way
of preserving their stock. If this is the case, it will
entail restraint in killing hen pheasants. You can't have
your cake and eat it. It may be reasonable to shoot
cocks into January, but the hens should be spared early
in the season. There is a prevalent habit on many rough
shoots of shooting too often. If the same ground is
covered on each occasion, once a fortnight is probably
all that the stock will stand. But there is another
consideration besides the mere depletion of the game.
In wild weather frequent shooting can drive the game off
the ground, and it may be lost for ever. One friend who
shoots approximately a thousand acres reserves his
pheasants for two days each season. He has a strong,
wild stock, and provides about fifty birds for his guests
on each occasion. There are, of course, other tactics by
which the shoot can be worked, spreading the sport over
many more enjoyable days, and I shall refer to these later.

In the meantime, it is perhaps sufficient to say that
a pheasant is not a very intelligent mother, and frequently fails to rear even half her eggs. Her enemies
are legion, and if the wild stock is not supported by
hand-reared birds it would probably be inadvisable to
shoot more than five out of every ten hens in residence
at the beginning of the season. The same proportions
might be roughly applied to partridges. Though they

are much better parents, their enemies are legion, too, and a larger stock than might appear necessary should be left at the end of each year. If the following spring is wet and cold, the losses among the eggs and young chicks may be so heavy that many pairs may fail to rear even a small family. The result is that we find ourselves among coveys of old birds which have banded together for company and give one a first, fleeting impression of strong, healthy families.

Rearing partridges, or re-stocking with French birds, is a problem outside the range of the amateur, and the ordinary tenant of a rough shoot. On the other hand, abandoned acres have been successfully restocked by artificial means, and the real enthusiast will find much to interest and encourage him if he is so minded.

The raising of a few pheasants is a different matter, and anyone who has kept hens has the basic knowledge on which to build. Good management, coupled with reasonable luck, should enable anyone to re-stock their covers at a cost of about five shillings a head. For every hundred eggs put under hens, eighty-five chicks represents a fair return, and of these perhaps sixty-five may finally reach the coverts in the late summer. Alternatively, the young birds may be purchased as poults and turned out into the woods, where regular feeding for the first week or two will persuade them that they have an attractive home.

It is not my intention to set out any of the methods of rearing which are commonly employed. They have been the subject of numerous expert publications, and such mention of the subject I have made is to suggest tentatively that, if the tenant's means permit, his duties as a sportsman call for their consideration. If this seems a reiteration of the obvious then I beg forgiveness, and make the excuse that each year sees additions to the ranks of the country-folk from the towns—men of goodwill who are great potential benefactors to our countryside.

CHAPTER VIII

WORKING THE SHOOT

"How are you going to work it?"

Joe regarded me with a benevolent twinkle which presaged something unusual, and which, no doubt, one or two of the guns grinding their boots on the sunlit gravel would eventually classify as outrageous. Joe was like that. When it was his turn to work the shoot he would hatch a plot which, given the weather, provided memorable sport. On some occasions, it was memorable because of our failure to bring down the rocketing pheasants, sent over so high and fast that they were barely possible. On others, it was a modest success with those high birds which sent everyone home with the conviction that we had the finest rough shoot in the county.

Anyone who bothered to count the bag knew it wasn't true. Joe's bags were often very small. When we entered them in the book at night Joe would look up and, still wearing his benevolent twinkle, would remark: "Pretty awful—but it was fun, wasn't it!"

When he spoke, I would see again the high, wild wings in the sky, the spirits of a swirling October day conjured from the crest of the top wood—something which nobody else would have thought of, and only Joe would have had the cheek to present. At such moments one knew that the success of a day was not measured by the size of the bag so much as by the quality of the shooting which went to making it.

"How are you going to work it to-day?"

Well—it began as most other days, with a walk through the stubbles, gathering a hare, a rabbit, and

flushing a covey of partridges which we hoped would
be met later in the roots on more even terms.

Then we came to the stream with the strip of wood
running beside it. It was boundary land, which meant
that it was a free-for-all, and no questions asked.
Thus a hen pheasant died a shattering death under a
barrage of lead which rendered its subsequent appearance on the table a gastronomical problem; later a
rabbit evacuated a thicket of brier, and a wood-pigeon
sailed serenely across the line of guns to meet a fusillade
which revealed the enthusiasm of the guests, if not the
quality of their judgement. It was a typical beginning
—though there were heart-burnings when Joe let past
a covey of partridge which rose from a hedge bottom.
Two young birds had been taken from it the previous
week.

So we came to the big ditch—a deep, overgrown
gully fenced on both sides by thorn and bramble, and
with sedges and willow by the water. We collected
here, and Joe's twinkle burst into flame again as he
said: "I think we'll give it a try."

The guests were blissfully ignorant of what was in
store for them, although the sight of the ditch, with its
matted undergrowth, obviously fired their imagination. Looking up its length, to where two high trees
stood sentinel at the further end, was to imagine scores
of pheasants, and even a wild duck or two, breaking
cover under the onslaught of the dogs. A rare titbit
for the rough shooter—a place to look back on at the
end of a hard day.

"You might go forward and post two guns in the
usual places," said Joe, with an unashamed wink.
"We'll take it up towards you—and if you see a hen,
well, have a bang at it!"

I knew what Joe meant, and as two of the guests
followed me I felt sorry for them. Even after I had
posted them on either side of the two trees (where they

were nicely hidden by a stone wall) I saw that they fancied their chances.

We then saw the remaining guns start up the ditch. They were slow, for the dogs needed to work every yard of it. The hedges combined with the undergrowth and made it hard work for them.

A pair of mallard broke cover, as I had hoped, and played true to form by climbing swiftly and coming down the line of the ditch high over the trees and barely within shot. The guests used four cartridges, and the duck went on, to melt into the hard blue sky.

Nothing happened for a while after that. But from past experience I knew that cocks and hens would be running up the ditch ahead of the dogs.

Then firing broke out in the distance—something to be expected, for the party had reached the break in the undergrowth where the cattle came to drink, a flush could always be relied upon here. In a second or two, three or four escaping forms were winging up the ditch. Behind the wall our guests got their guns ready, crouching like conspirators.

The birds came low, six or eight feet up, and as they flew down-wind they were moving fast. It looked as though they were to offer a nice shot. Then fifty yards away the usual happened. The birds put up their elevators and climbed like fighters making for the clouds. For no clear reason, save that they always did it at this place, they turned themselves into one of the most sporting shots that our shoot has to offer— and the guests missed. I felt particularly pleased, because I got an old cock from my position fifty yards back in the plough behind the trees.

Maybe it was ungenerous of me to take this station, for the game levelled out after their sensational climb and the extra dimension was taken out of the aiming problem. Yet the shots which had been offered were better than mine and perfectly possible. As we liked to show our visitors attractive shooting I had no compunction.

Ten birds were eventually collected, but seven were killed by the walkers. Of the other three, the visitors had a brace, and were full of apologies for what they considered bad shooting. They didn't know that we had put first-class shots in that position with little more result.

We were "doing the bowl" that day, and these preliminary moves were shifting the game towards the top wood. The bowl lay on its farther side, created by a deformity of the earth's crust which had formed the sweeping curves of a basin lined with the softest and sweetest green turf. The wind would be blowing clear over the top of it to-day, giving the guests the impression that the stiff breeze had died, while in truth it was blowing furiously far overhead. The pheasants would be flying in it, and their speed over the ground would not be less than sixty miles an hour. Thus it was when we came to the place about noon. Not one of the half-circle of guns standing in the hollow felt more than a breath of air upon his cheek and, looking upwards to the crescent trees, imagination ran away with us as we pictured the high pheasants breasting the tops.

It had been pretty work on Joe's part, and not alone on account of his success in working the game into that windy sanctuary. His timing was equally praiseworthy, his organisation and his tact as well. We had beaters, cajoled by honeyed words to give up some of their lunch-hour. They came pouring from the rusty red buildings which lay under the horn of the crescent—ploughmen and boys, men from the potato-fields and the cow-byre, and with them came the farmer, powerfully armed with a pair of Damascus barrels and his pockets bulging with cartridges.

The beaters went round the farther slope, striking

the full force of the wind on the crest, so that the observant ones saw that their trouser legs were flapping about their ankles. The farmer stayed, broad-smiling, and with a friendly nod for the gentlemen with whom he was unacquainted.

"You were in nice time," he said, wishing to compliment Joe on keeping his appointment to the minute. "The lads'll be round directly."

It was indeed nice to see how smoothly the plans were maturing. As the rattle of sticks upon trunks came down to us from beyond the rise, scarcely five minutes after taking our places, it was clear that once again Joe had deserved well of us. I looked along the half-circle within the walls of the basin, each man standing with legs apart and shoulders back as he watched the high skyline ahead. A springer splashed his lovely chocolate-and-cream coat against the emerald of the grass; a big Labrador, blacker than night, sat at his master's feet beyond. My own dog whimpered anxiously, turning her great brown eyes from my own to the crest of ridge. The stage was set.

The first pheasant came with a rattle of wings from the centre of the crescent. She was a lone hen, and appeared to mount into the sky as she came forward. We were standing about eighty yards from the edge of the wood, and by the time she was over us I think she was as many feet high.

A gun cracked, and to everyone's astonishment, including the man who fired, the lady curled up in the air and came tumbling out of the sky with the suddenness of a falling star. The body hit the ground with a thump and a cloud of feathers. A dog streaked like a flash to pick it up thirty yards back, and as his mouth closed a second pheasant came from the trees.

There was no time to look at the dogs now, or wonder how others were faring: pheasants broke into the skyline in threes and fours, gathered speed, and came into range so high overhead that every shot was a vertical shot, and a second barrel was an exercise for the back muscles seldom encountered in a day's sport. Out of the corner of an eye I saw many birds go on, but now and again one crumpled and somersaulted, falling earthwards, to hit the ground seconds later.

It didn't last long—perhaps seven or eight minutes. Not more than fifty birds crossed our line, and probably a dozen less. But every one of us had had some superb chances, and every gun except my own was claiming a bird as the dogs ran hither and thither on the pick-up. If seven hen pheasants and four cocks seem a small result for the big event of the day, it was voted by everyone as satisfactory. The quality was certainly there, even though the quantity was lacking. Nor were eleven birds a poor return for the cartridges expended. Joe had been wont to produce a stock apology after this event. "I'm afraid they were out of range," he would say. To-day he was silent, but the smile on his face was the testimony of his pleasure.

The old farmer breathed huskily into my ear as he departed. He had collected three birds, and was taking one of them home with him. "Mon," he said, "I've seen more birds come out of yon wood—but I've niver seen 'em higher nor faster, and I've niver seen 'em shot better." Tribute indeed!

We went down to the bog after lunch. Sooner or later we paid it a visit on most shooting days, for it had all those qualities which appeal to the vagabond with a gun.

It grew out of the groin of the valley, subtly and secretly so that one hardly knew where it began. At first the tilled earth gave place to grass, with here and there a sprout of marsh-grass, a bed of marigolds, and spongy patches of moss. Then the valley widened and flattened, and the tilled land was left as the bog came into its own. Now the stream broke out of its channel and spread its tentacles through a forest of tall and brittle rushes. It made black ditches for itself, and the rushes hid them, so that for nearly a quarter of a mile there was a treacherous wilderness.

Yet even here the alder and the brier and the willow survived, and sprung forth on every patch of harder ground, to create a thicket. So the bog was not all bog, and within at least two of its curious, thicket-infested humps rabbits had established their burrows. About the centre there was a chain of small pools, and as the winter rains swelled their size, and the gales blew out of the north-east, the duck would come in. They would sit during the day, and such was the excellence of the cover that a shot was possible if one took the trouble to approach upwind.

We had scarcely left behind the pasture when a wisp of snipe offered a chance, and then another and another, until we had seen at least a score of them. It was curious how a high wind and a douche of rain would bring them in. For weeks there would never be a sign of them, and then for a month we were almost persuaded that we had a real snipe bog—which wasn't true.

With a leash safely in the bag, we ploughed on, to rouse a heron from the gutter which fed into the first of the pools. An old mallard got up out of shot, but the hen bird sat closer and was collected by a lucky shot from fifty yards. There should have been partridge in the wilderness of drier ground fringing the northern side; but we probably moved too fast and walked over them. They would sit as tight as cock pheasants, and it was difficult to teach an eager guest that he must turn himself into a human ferret if he was to make the best of it.

Then the inevitable happened. Into one of the narrow, watery man-traps a guest disappeared. We heard the splash and the choking protest. A cock pheasant chose the moment to break out of the under-growth within a couple of yards—a well-timed retreat. If Joe had not always placed business first it would have escaped. As it was, he dealt with the old gentlemen quite mercilessly, and then attended to his guest. Assistance was invariably needed on these occasions, for even the most athletic found the combination of sticky mud and water, waist-deep, and always very cold, beyond their unaided powers.

The line paused while Joe did the honours, no doubt thankful for the chance of a short rest. I could see their guns sticking up like poles here and there over the high reeds. Only in one place was a complete shooter in view—a refugee on an island a few feet high.

We moved on again, and in a moment were among the real wealth of the bog—a dozen pheasants in almost as many yards, driven one by one from thickets of dwarf willow, silver birch, and matted undergrowth. At the farther side of it a woodcock flickered silently ahead of us, to be pursued by a hail of shot, and go on untouched. More water followed, and as we plunged ahead we came to the part occupied by the coots— along the banks of the stream which was once again gathering itself into a proper channel. We let them go, and so came to the end of it on a hard, sandy track mounted on a ridge and leading to the pastures up the hill. Here we gathered like truant puppies, each carrying our spoils.

Seven pheasants were counted, three rabbits, a couple of snipe and a duck. It was a fair finish to a typical day.

How are you going to work it ?

The answer, of course, has been resolved since the "host" went out of doors to feel the wind and look at the sky. If it was a dewy morning, bright and still, with a touch of frost—a promise of one of those

The country of the Red Deer. *See page* 145.

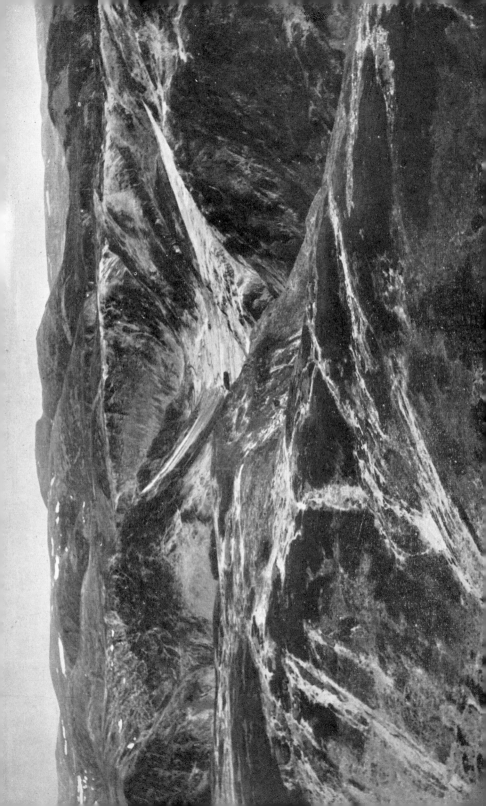

The formation breaks as the gunner fires. At the bottom left of the picture, denoted by arrow, a goose is falling.

glorious September days which will warm up towards noon, and the whole sky fill with snowy fair-weather cumulus—then the answer will be different from the day which tried to get through the front door on a blast of wind out of a hard sky. The answer may be different again when Joe is "working the shoot," while if yet another friend—a good shot and a wise man—were to be asked, there would be a third plan in the making.

The truth is—and this is a personal opinion—a shoot can be handled in several different ways under identical conditions. The plans can be designed to produce the greatest possible bag in a given number of hours, or a smaller bag for which the plan is the same but the technique different; or lastly, a bag which is made up of birds which have been a pleasure and a thrill to shoot.

I remember a day when Joe again was in charge, and I found myself standing thirty yards back from a strip of wood waiting for partridges, which were to come almost as high and as fast as pheasants. Once more my partner had used all his craft in bringing the birds into a big root-field on the far side of the strip. The wind, and a pair of flanking guns, made it possible to lift the partridges over the high trees so that they came at the guns like driven hail. This was the kind of shooting we preferred.

If shooters who have concentrated on large bags turn to such considerations they will open new avenues of pleasure for themselves and their friends. When game is wanted, it is not difficult to get if it is on the ground. Sometimes one will pass over game intentionally, working the ground lightly, and preferring to leave for another day game which might have been had if required. But more often I have been a member of a party which has passed through a patch of rough, hoping for partridges and pheasants and a few rabbits, and emerged from the thickets and the long grass

I

disappointed, firmly believing that there was nothing there. The truth is that the line has moved too fast. Impatience is a modern trait, and it is seen at its worst in such places as these.

None of this is to deny the principles by which a shoot is organised. One does not deliberately drive game off the ground by walking up fields towards the boundary, or beat the coverts in the face of a gale. But, leaving the obvious aside, there are often opportunities for improving the bag which are lost through a lack of understanding of the likes and dislikes of the game— and consequently their whereabouts at any particular moment. When the wind is cold, but the sun shining, it is often the shallow bowl in the field of stubble which shelters a covey of partridges. The birds like the warmth and hate the wind. By the same token, all sheltered slopes, whether on open or rough ground, are usually more fruitful then those which are exposed. Again, one cannot shoot for long without realising that partridges have instincts in common with their pursuers. They don't like the drip of water on to their backs from the leaves of the roots, and so they will not voluntarily resort to them in a downpour. Nor do they like facing a high wind and, as we know to our cost, they are liable to scatter over the heads of the beaters like chaff. On the other hand, they are as conscious as we are of the charms of home sweet home, and where a partridge has been born and bred there it will stay, unless some enthusiastic amateur persists in harrying its quarters in a gale of wind, or shoots late into the afternoon, during the hour of its evening meal on the stubbles.

These are some of the elementary considerations of any plan. They will lead to decisions which will vary with the strength and direction of the wind. They will all probably lead to a walk through the stubbles in the morning with the general idea of concentrating the stock in the largest and most convenient area of roots.

The birds which may be so wild on a windy October day that a fair shot in the open is unlikely will at least give a chance from the cover. Yet even this general plan may be subject to other considerations, for I remember only too well a day when I believed I had chosen wisely, only to be reminded that there are roots and roots. We had taken a long stubble towards a commodious and promising-looking field which I ought to have remembered was ninety per cent. sugar-beet with a narrow strip of turnips on its farther side. It was the intention to divide the party at the roots, one half to drive the field towards the remainder, who were to line the down-wind end next to the turnips. As we began to take our places it was revealed that the four coveys which we had so carefully shepherded had all pitched in the turnips twenty yards ahead of us. Partridges do not like sugar-beet—at least not when there are turnips next door. We should have done better to have walked the stubble against the wind towards a field of well-grown clover.

But before any plan is conceived, the first consideration is whether the ground is to be walked or driven. Driven birds usually give better shooting, and pheasants walked-up in roots sometimes give no shooting at all. In the early part of the season, when the tops are thick, they often rise so close that the occasion is not even a sporting event.

When beaters have not been available we have often divided the party into two sections. It may be a dangerous proceeding among an assembly of careless guns. Two lines of shooters, one concealed behind a hedge, the other, equally aggressively minded, walking towards them, provide a stage for an unpleasant accident. Yet this method is becoming more popular, and, amongst those who are accustomed to it, an attitude of mind is developed which is an insurance against accidents.

There is the other sort of shooting occasion which is replete with disasters through the fault of the shooters themselves. Generally there is one particular culprit, devoid of "field sense," who sartorially looks like a shooter, but whose resemblance goes no further. It is worth parading an example, on the chance that some-one will hang his head in shame and perhaps reform.

The day dawned frosty and fine, with the prospect of shooting fifteen hundred acres lying in a valley beside a lovely river. There were crisp stubbles and dark pine-woods, a bog, and a sweep of heather falling from the higher ground. We were to take the stubbles in the morning, driving them into a big acreage of roots lying along the line of a wood. To this end, a few beaters had been mustered, and as we stood on the lawn of our host's house, in the sunshine of the early morning, the prospect was fair indeed. After the stubbles we were to walk the roots, leaving the pheasants to go into the wood, and reserving them for the big drive of the day.

"But first," said our host, "we'll have a shot at the duck. There are a few native mallard in the swamp, and it's all on the way."

So off we went, down through the woods, until the swamp lay below—a wilderness of scrub, reeds, and flood water, enclosed by the gleaming shingle of the river, and backed on its farther side by a substantial belt of trees. The beaters were to go round and come down into the swamp by the trees, bringing whatever there might be on to the water over our heads.

As we took our places in silence outside the swamp, each of us screened by a bush, the omens were pro-pitious. Somewhere, far out ahead, an old drake squawked. It was the signal for the trouble-makers to open their campaign. The man on my right, a guest in an impeccable suiting, who was carrying a gun worth every penny of a hundred guineas, called out in a rich, penetrating voice—the sort of voice which can be such an asset at more distinguished gatherings —inquiring whether I had heard. I had—and so also had a duck which happened to be lying some fifty yards ahead. She rose from the reeds with a clatter of wings and made out over the scrub towards the open water and the beaters. I waited in breathless silence for further results, and in a few moments they came. A chorus of squawking preceded a rise of a dozen mallard from the open water. They circled, climbing fast, saw the beaters, who were beginning to line out beyond the belt of trees, and came back above our heads. The impenitent sportsman on my right opened fire as they passed over out of shot.

"By gad, they were high!" he called out cheerfully.

Twenty minutes later we were marching along a hedgerow bounding one of the stubble-fields which were to be driven towards us. We were within five minutes of taking our places behind the hedge at the end of the same field when an animated conversation broke out between my late companion and a second guest. A moment later I saw through a gap in the hedge a covey of partridge running as though their lives depended on it. They were about fifty yards away, and the chances were that they would have remained sitting in the warm sun had they not been disturbed. I hoped that our host wouldn't notice them, but a moment later I saw him walking back along the line to speak to the transgressors. I caught the drift of apologies in a loud voice, and felt sure that now our troubles would be over. We could stand the loss of a brace of duck and a covey of partridges without serious injury to our enjoyment. But little did any of us realise what our fellow-shooters had remaining in their repertoire.

After each of us had been posted by our host there were two significant movements on the part of the guns.

In each instance, it was one from a thick part of the hedge to a thinner and lower part, where the head and shoulders of the two shooters were clear of the cover. Personally, I didn't mind, because I happened to be next to one of the two men, and his changed position merely meant that I was likely to enjoy more shooting. This is exactly what happened. The birds divided on seeing the animated sportsmen levelling their weapons: they sheered off, and streamed over the guns on either side. After the drive, one of the men said to the other: "Bad luck, old man—'fraid the birds didn't come our way that time."

Some of this will be hard to credit. Yet it is no caricature, and being fairly launched on my tale I propose to finish it. The ensuing episode was a ten-minute delay in the root-field while one of the guns insisted on looking for a winged bird. He made a personal search, fouling the scent for his dog, which ranged far and wide, and putting up another covey forty yards away. In the meantime, every partridge in the vicinity was given time to collect its wits, run forward, and make good its escape along the ditch which bounded the field. That a proportion of the birds availed themselves of the opportunity was evident from the results over the rest of the ground.

The final debacle was staged by the same gun after lunch. Sent round with another guest to take up a flanking position at the corner of the wood, he fired four cartridges at pigeons on the way, and rounded off the work by killing a rabbit as it sought the shelter of the trees. Speaking of it afterwards, his companion —who I happen to know never carries a loaded gun between stands—remarked wryly that the shooting had been extraordinarily good. Three wood-pigeons had been collected.

And the result? It is difficult to be certain. But it was significant that the ensuing drive produced only one cock against more than twenty hens. It might have been due to inefficient beating—but a better argument is that the cannonade at close quarters had started a forced march on the part of those extremely wily male birds.

Nobody deliberately initiates disasters of this sort, and ignorance is, of course, at the root of the matter. Unfortunately, those who take up shooting late in life have not had the advantage of a stern parent or a keeper to instil the elements of discipline. Equally unfortunately, the late-comer to the field is unduly sensitive about his ignorance, as though he felt it ill-bred to admit that he didn't know everything required of him. He will accept a lesson at golf from an expert friend, but he will merely grow red in the face if the same is suggested to him in the field.

CHAPTER IX

PIGEONS

THE mist was creeping up the sides of the red cliffs. It came in slow, gentle puffs on an east wind and billowed inland until the standing grain, the roots, the stone walls, and the distant line of trees were robbed of their identity one by one. The sea looked no more than a mirage from the top of the cliffs—a blue-grey smudge lit by the white wing-tips of the gulls a hundred feet below.

I was not far away from the Red Head, and directly above the sea-tunnel leading under a big field. I was after rock-pigeons, and sat watching them flickering like ghosts along the face of the cliff. They were playing a game of follow-my-leader which began out in the mist and ended deep under the cliff when they hurtled into the tunnel. They flew its subterranean length for a hundred yards or so, and then zoomed upwards in a sensational climb, and so out of the hole in the ground in the middle of the field.

I tried a couple of shots, but when a bird fell like a plummet into the sea, from where it was impossible to recover, I gave it up, and found more pleasure in watching them. They are brilliant on the wing and have a trick of flying full speed over the edge of the cliff from the landward side, and dropping vertically to the crests of the waves. It was a manœuvre which is beyond the capabilities of any human aerobatic, for its negative " G " would bring the red blood into the pilot's eyes and render him unconscious in half a second. I think it is executed by a sudden flexing of the wings which gives them negative incidence, although the suddenness of the descent is suggestive of a high-speed stall. I know of no other bird which takes such a delight in manœuvres of this kind.

When they tired of playing follow-my-leader they bunched into close formation and went swinging along the face of the cliffs, rising and falling in the air currents, banking in steep turns and displaying an airmanship which would have done credit to a fulmar petrel. Yet it is a curious thing that they rarely rode on the cliff airs as a gull will ride. In a wind of more than ten miles an hour there was always a vertical current over the crests which would carry a gull to twice their height—a vertical element of perhaps five feet per second. But the rock-pigeons preferred to keep their " motors " running, and would fall away from the cliff-top where the lift was powerful to dive sensationally for the sea, and then, using their speed to climb again, would rise to their former level before skirting the rock face at perilous proximity.

Whatever the relationship between these pigeons and their brothers of the woods, their characters are so different that they might belong to another species. The wood-pigeon is an individualist. He has no sense of rhythm, and when he flies in company his formation is ragged and without geometric form. The rock-pigeon, on the other hand, is a member of an indivisible community, flying out on his sorties as a drilled squadron, whether in quest of food or sport.

Lying in the short wire grass of the cliff-tops, I have caught the sense of delight which so clearly in-spires their aerial displays, and when they rocket at full speed into the mouth of a cave, or hurtle through such a tunnel as the one under the big field, I have sensed their exhilaration at doing something dangerous. A few of them appear to have interbred with domestic varieties, for as a formation has swung below I have often noticed strange and unorthodox markings. I came to know one bird which was pure white save for light brown wing-tips, and another which was a glossy black—as dark as a raven. Yet the cross-breds were of a size with their fellows, perhaps two-thirds of the weight of a wood-pigeon.

They are to be found along the high cliffs, wherever there are caves where they can build their nests. On my part of the coast the country people net the caves, a ruthless method of catching them for the market, but perhaps the only practical way of obtaining them in any numbers. As a sporting quarry for a man with a gun they are the equal of many better-known birds, demanding a standard of shooting which makes a small bag worth the effort.

It was a long time before I found a satisfactory way of shooting them. The cliffs were in most places unscaleable, so that even when the pigeons didn't fall into the sea they lay out on some ledge which could not be reached without a boat. The problem was to place myself so that the birds fell on accessible land. One method was to mark a point of the cliff which a particular colony had formed the habit of crossing on its way to the fields to feed. They would use the same place time after time, so that when I perched myself (usually precariously) just below the lip there was a chance of half a dozen shots in the course of an afternoon. The speed of their flight, and the necessity to shoot so far in front that they fell on the cliff-top, made a brace for the pot a satisfactory return.

But the photograph on page 112 (which shows the tunnel in the cliffs leading to the hole in the big field) also illustrates the place where I at last found the best shooting. I noticed that the birds when at play took a delight in racing along the light patch of shingle, and then rising steeply, to cross the narrow neck of land which runs out to the great rock standing seawards. They came over the crest like driven grouse, fast and low, and by lying full length on my back under the crest of the peninsula I had a skyline twenty-five yards away, and an instant in which to shoot. It entailed the fastest shooting I have ever attempted, for there was no warning whatever that the birds were coming. The empty skyline was suddenly filled with advancing wings and unless one of them was stopped within a dozen yards its momentum would carry its body across the peninsula and into the sea. I never succeeded in getting off a second barrel, but by holding the gun to the shoulder with the safety catch down—a tiring position—I sometimes had half a dozen birds to take home. It was a curious thing that the same formation would cross the narrow neck three or four times before it realised that one of its number was being shot down on each circuit.

The case of the rock-pigeons was another instance of a roundabout way of obtaining sport. By waiting for them on their feeding grounds they were easier to shoot and there were more chances. But the quality of the chances bore no comparison with those swift moments on the cliff-tops. In a farmyard near by was a hen run, rectangular in shape, and enclosed on three sides by a stone wall. At certain times of the year, when there was a shortage of grain on the ground, they would come in and join the hens at their afternoon meal. A quiet approach behind the wall would sometimes bring a score of them into view twenty yards away, with probably half a dozen wood-pigeons, fatter and lighter coloured, strutting amongst them. One day the farmer bagged six with one shot—and a hen !

I sometimes found them among the grain before it was cut, feeding in a little gold-framed oasis of corn which had been laid by the wind. As it meant approaching through the standing crop one's interest was usually academic. But on the several occasions when I was able to make a stalk without doing damage it was interesting to observe that the sound of the wind among the ears made it possible to come quite close from the down-wind side. I never understood this, for when wood-pigeons are roosting in trees it needs almost a full gale to conceal the sound of an intruder.

Later in the year the pigeons haunted the stacks, and there can be few shooters who have not taken advantage of their cover when out for a wood-pigeon. A hide burrowed into the side of the stack generally paid a dividend as soon as it was definitely ascertained that the birds were feeding there. To make the hide casually and without previous reconnaissance was generally a waste of time. For reasons best known to themselves, the feeding grounds were changed suddenly and sometimes without apparent reason. For weeks the stacks would be deserted.

In the days when business took me each morning over the North Sea—days when the sea was without ships, and the most one could hope for companionship was a fleeting glimpse of a flight of duck—I used to spend many of the winter evenings in quest of pigeons for the pot. If I wasn't too late home I would catch them as they came in from the fields to the woods, and generally a particular member of my squadron would accompany me. This fellow-shooter almost came into the category of a first-class shot, which is to say that for every ten cartridges he fired during a day's walking after partridges or pheasants he could be expected to produce nine birds, and when the game was driven his average was very little lower. He was certainly the most artistic performer with whom I have shot regularly. But the pigeons for which we used to wait in the clearings of the woods discovered his weakness— and it is a weakness which is common to many men who are otherwise very good.

One evening, when a south-east wind was bringing in a mist from the sea, we took up our stands fifty yards apart in a ditch which lined the edge of a steepling

wood of beech and Scotch fir. It was a favourite place
for both ourselves and the pigeons and it was a poor
night when the opportunities did not account for
twenty cartridges. On the other hand, if we came away
with ten birds between us we considered that we had
done well.

To-night the mist was writhing among the tree-
tops. The interval between hearing the sound of wings
and seeing the birds was a short one, for pigeons, like
the rest of us, have a poor stomach for blind flying.
The result was a most suggestive improvement in the
ratio of cartridges to kills. My friend seemed to regain
all his old form, while I—certainly missing more birds
—felt pleased with myself.

" I know what I have been doing," said my companion, as we joined forces again. " I've been shooting
at them out of range."

A statement which had so obvious a ring about it
may not appear to be worth remarking. Yet I am sure
that many people who have a nice judgement of range
on other occasions are hopelessly at fault when flighting
wood-pigeons. It is a fault which has led to the popular
use of No. 4 shot, not because the shooter believes that
the birds are a long way off, but because he thinks that
they are " tough." It is fours, he will tell you, which
will bring them down. And so they will, because these
pellets retain sufficient velocity to kill at twenty yards
greater range than sixes. The fact that the pattern
is inadequate to ensure a hit is disregarded, on the
reasonable grounds that the smaller shot produces
still less satisfactory results.

In our case it required a heavy mist to remind us of
the greater truth. The birds were flying only just over
the tree-tops at between seventy and ninety feet from
the ground, whereas on fine evenings they were mostly
over a hundred feet high and at such an angle that they
were either out of range altogether or flying through a

hopelessly scattered pattern. The pigeons above these high trees seemed less difficult when I used my wild-fowling gun, which is fully choked in both barrels and chambered for three-inch cartridges. A load of No. 4 shot from this gave a reasonable pattern as well as the necessary velocity to bring the pigeons down whenever it was held straight.

I think that most shooters regard their pigeon-shooting too lightly. It is taken as an afterthought to a day in the coverts or over the stubbles which has finished early, and sometimes as an evening's pastime to be classed in the category of taking the dog for a walk. In fact, it can provide a test of shooting which is often not discovered during the length of an organised day. As a type of shooting which can be obtained by anyone for the asking (I have never known a farmer who didn't welcome me wherever I have been) it is worth some thought, and the more so because of the difficult shots it offers. On these grounds, the con-struction of a brushwood hide, or at the least a piece of camouflage netting to drape over the hat, is as obvious as it is, in fact, rare.

The eyesight of a pigeon is remarkable, and when it is approaching its home wood it is searching the ground for the least sign of unnatural movement. A few square inches of human face peering through a bush is detectable at more than two hundred yards. From this point of view its capabilities rank with those of a wild duck. On the other hand, it is difficult to correlate this with the effectiveness of a decoy which is set out in the stubble where the birds have been known to be feeding. A dead bird, with its head propped up by a twig, and turned facing into wind, is obviously dead to a human being, Why should it deceive a superior pair of eyes? I suppose the answer must be contained in the pigeon's psychology. A few scattered feathers from the decoy, or the footmarks of the shooter, are more likely to prevent the birds coming down.

A wood which I have often shot is shown in the photograph on page 97. It was here that the ordinary tactics of waiting for the birds to flight in might be vastly improved by having a second gun concealed in the opposing strip. It was possible, at least for a while, to run a shuttle service between the two woods. Those originally disturbed in the first went across to the second, and vice versa, while the new-comers from the fields were equally obliging. Finally, of course, the pigeon population sought other refuges for the night.

If, instead, one walked into these strips alone, with no more camouflage than a hat, the opportunities of shots within range were more than halved. There were some rhododendron bushes in which it was possible to submerge oneself, but the skyline ahead was open for sixty or seventy yards. It was rare for a pigeon to come straight on over the trees if one's face was un-covered. One might have supposed that in good cover, such as is revealed by the photograph, camouflage or special hides could be dispensed with. It was never true. It never can be true where wood-pigeons are shot regularly.

CHAPTER X

THE FOREST

THE forest begins at the end of the road—where the ordinary things of life leave off. The last village, the last house, and the last cultivated field, with its crumbling stone wall, lies behind. The road twists and climbs among the foot-hills, and becomes a heather-covered track before it crosses the last bridge over the dwindling burn, to be swallowed at the door of an empty bothy. This is a treeless world, a confusion of rock and heather, cliff and cloud shadow steeped in silence. It has the power to raise the human spirit as though to a challenge, or depress it as though it were imprisoned. After nightfall, it is a place where Christian would have drawn his sword.

Yet if you spend long enough in its wilderness it emerges with a personality and a surprisingly large population. The distant pinnacles and the barren high-tops, only to be reached sweat-soaked on a hot September day, reveal themselves as the home of ptarmigan, grouse, hawks, eagles, larks, ring-ouzels, and above all, the red deer.

I have looked down upon the forest when I have been flying at a great height—speculatively, as a new angel might regard a corner of the mortal kingdom over which he may be asked to keep watch. Like most other things looked at from an angel's angle, the view is instructive. Height robs the mountains of their dignity, reducing them to the single dimension of a level plain. But it also shows the forest as different from all other places. It is without pattern, except the aimless pattern of a designer who has lost his wits.

And it is darker than the places in which we live ourselves. Blue-black, purple, and grey-blue shapes lie
among patches of russet-brown, burnt umber, and
sickly ochre. Looking down one sees instantly that it
is unbowed to discipline, without regiment. From this
height it seems, too, to be a dead place. There is no
drift of city smoke to lend the illusion of life ; no road,
no crawling speck by which the charabanc announces
itself to the airman, no roof of bright colour, no sign
of man's sovereignty. Yet as I have swung the sombre
patchwork around me, sliding back the cockpit hood
to let the ice-cold air stream over my head, I have
traced the silver veins of its burns and felt that the mass
might be a sleeping monster—a monster that lives so
slowly that to livers like ourselves it appears dead.

Commercially, it is not of much use to mankind.
The darker patches are crumbling seams of black peat,
the purples and grey-blues are igneous rock erupting
through the russet and umber shades of the heather,
while the lighter colours are the mountain grass upon
which the deer feed. It is a poor enough wilderness,
fit only for a few Cheviot and Blackface sheep along its
fringes during the summer months. Yet it has the one
characteristic demanded by the red deer for existence—
freedom from the sight, scent, and sound of man and all
his works. For this a stag will graze the mountain-
sides, following the young grass upwards towards the
high-tops as the summer advances. Given fine weather
in August, he may not descend below two thousand
feet until the first storms of autumn drive him off the
peaks. Only in the depth of winter can hunger drive
him into the fringes of civilisation—to the furthermost
field where he can rob some upland farmer of a square
meal.

He is, perhaps, the last true member of the wild of
any size to survive the dominance of the master race
within our shores. He is banished from the English

K

shires, driven north from the lowlands, driven from forest to forest to ever higher ground, till he is left only the waste places at whose gates the masses are already clamouring. It has been a retreat before a horde which has spoiled, burned, soiled, and civilised. The canopy of trees which once spread from the Solway to the Pentland Firth has gone. Had men looked down from balloon or aeroplane in the twelfth century they would have looked upon such a land of trees as they could match to-day only in the jungles of the tropics. Not one-twentieth of the surface is now so clothed. From the pinnacle of time, they might have seen the deer-hunt in full cry across the plains of Fife and on the fringes of the modern Glasgow, in the lowlands of Ettrick, Kirkcudbright, and Stirling. But as the centuries passed, carrying with them the illustrious roll of English kings, each of whom almost without exception regarded sport in the forests as one of the more precious perquisites of the Crown, the deer retreated. The middle of the last century found them in their ultimate fortress, and here for the moment they remain. Nor, unless these final gates are stormed, need their numbers grow less. For other things beside the trees have departed. The wolves have gone, the practice of driving deer with half a thousand beaters has gone, the deer-hounds have gone, and in some places even the poachers have gone. What is left is a single man with a rifle and a world of mountain solitudes. Maybe it is a kingdom which is yet destined for the rape of progress. But it is so poor a kingdom that there is a chance yet of the last stag escaping the fate of so many who have gone before him—a place in the cage of a metropolitan Zoo.

In the meantime, there is still this lonely figure with a rifle, and still the classic beast to offer him a worthy challenge. Indeed, the deer are more wary than they have been in their long history, and beside the eyes and

the legs of a man, which need to be in good order, there
is a greater requirement for a profound instinct of the
chase. What other beast can scent his hunter at a
thousand yards, catching a wind-borne breath as faint
as the whiff of the distant sea, yet strong enough to
send him reeling back on to his haunches as though
struck by a bullet? What other beast will come to the
hour-old track of a man, to turn and bolt like a terrified
horse. Even the shadow of an eagle which soars the
slope wind may clear a glen, and the rattle of wings
from a covey of grouse disturbed by a stalker may put
a herd upon the move.

Three thousand feet high, at the head of a remote
burn, a man built a hut so that he might spend the
nights upon the hills, and so be ready on the high-tops
again when the sun rose. He was young and enthusiastic, and chose the place because in the prevalent
wind it was the custom of the deer to come this way.
The hut proved its worth on the first day, and again
on the second day. But within a week the herds knew
that there was a foreigner in the glen, and they deserted
it. There was not enough room in the vast stretches
of hag and heather for the deer and a single member
of the human race. There is never enough room for
a flock of sheep and their shepherd, or even a big
population of grouse and their occasional shooters.
I was last in the hut a year ago, untenanted for a decade,
sides bulging, door broken, and while I sat on what
had once been a table its builder told me its story.

Is it to be wondered that the stalking of such a
beast is rated high among the sports? As I ask myself
that question I see in my mind's eye a small herd
gathered in a pass between two hills, with the prospect
of an easy stalk over the opposing ridge, and when I
propound it to the man at my side I hear his voice
again saying that—yon beasts will be safe enough from
us that day. They had chosen a place where two

winds were blowing—airs divided by the hills to give warning from both directions.

No wonder, perhaps, it is customary to bow to such sagacity and, however effete it may seem, to employ a professional stalker. There can scarcely be one amateur in five who knows the tricks of his forest well enough to come up with his own beast. If we are honest, we must admit that under the guidance of our professionals we are doing little more than to demonstrate our endurance, our ability to crawl, and lastly our capacity for hitting a comparatively large target at short range with a high-power rifle. We who are able to stalk our own trout, and gaff our own salmon, may find it a trifle galling. To have a rifle thrust into our hands, to be told to take a particular beast, firing high or low, depending upon the fall of the ground, is not all we would wish of a sport. Yet so often there is no other choice, and in acknowledging that the stag is our master, we may at least watch and admire the skill of the man in front. A wiser and tougher breed of sportsmen exist nowhere else in the world, and whenever I have heard men talking of the beasts they have grassed in the forest I think of the silent, unacknowledged folk who have made it possible.

. . . .

I saw my first herd of red deer on a green mountain-side in June. The grass of the high-tops was not yet grown, and both stags and hinds had left the calves to come down and graze on the more luscious grass of the lower slopes. I was fishing the upper reaches of a Highland river, and in the late evening light I thought that the deer had not seen me. Yet when I put up my rod, and mounted the bank, I saw myself returning the indifferent stare of a stag not more than three hundred yards away. It was the shattering of my first illusion—that red deer are always unapproachable.

Late that same year, in the frost of a winter afternoon, I stood in a woodland clearing and saw the head stalker throw back his head to give birth to an unearthly call—a sound which he assured me would bring the deer down from the hills. After a few minutes I saw a head raised above the purple skyline of the opposing slope, and then another and another. Soon the whole hill grew into life through the smoky shadows of bounding forms coming towards us. After twenty minutes, while we waited concealed and in silence, the first beast parted the shadows of a bush fifty yards away and came into the clearing. For a moment he stood irresolute, as a girl might stand on the edge of a ballroom floor at her first dance. Then lowering his proud head, dismissing the anxieties of the shadows in which we were hidden, he began to feed on the maize spread generously over the pine-needles. In another few minutes the clearing was filled with stags. Another delusion had gone—that the red deer were always without domestic qualities.

Again, one wild October day on the road to Skye, where the mountains tumble in to the folds of Glen Shiel, I came round a bend and found myself face to face with a stag twenty yards away. The bold look in his eye—the wild, purposeful look of the rutting stag before his belly falls away and he assumes an aspect of debauchery—gave more than a hint of immediate battle. This was no retiring fawn of picture-book tradition, but a male warrior accoutred in all his armour, and in no mood for compromise. Yet was I, the king of the universe, to move off the road for him? The impasse was resolved at the beast's leisure, when, after staring insolently, he gave me the right of way. The last delusion was gone—that man must always be the hunter and the red deer the hunted.

The deer we know with affection is neither the harmless beast of June who shows himself in search of the better lowland grass, nor the domineering, sex-crazed, and highly scented warrior of mid-October. Nor is he the half-starved skeleton who leaves his kingdom for a man-provided dinner in the dead of winter which he eats within a stone's-throw of a curious sightseer. He is the fleet-footed, elusive spirit of the hills, moving with his herd across the high-tops, hearkening only to the call and the warning of the wind. Now he is the athlete in perfect condition. His very mien is a challenge to the hunter to do his damnedest.

We sat on the top of a flat rock, eating our sandwiches. From our backs blew a gentle wind, carrying our scent up the glen, so that had any deer lain closely in its path they must have bolted. But we had already examined the ground through our glasses, and though we had seen a small herd grazing on the hill-side about two thousand yards away, the intervening slopes were bare. In any case, it was of no serious moment, for it was the first of August and we were unarmed. The sun and the high air and the prospect of the mountains had brought us into the forest—to see what we could see.

We had trained the telescope on the herd, and noted the thick horns of a stag in velvet, and another with strips hanging from his points like untidy ribbons. In another month, or perhaps less, both beasts would be worthy of stalking. In the meantime, it was our pleasure to watch them, unaware of our presence.

When the sandwiches were finished we lit our pipes, and my companion lay on his back on the rock in the sun. He was content, he said, to watch the clouds chase each other across the blue sky. I, on the other hand, watched the deer through the telescope, I trained it on a hind whose calf was lying on a green runner within a few paces of her. She was grazing up-wind, head towards me. But as I watched she suddenly stiffened, raised her head, and danced backwards as I've seen a frightened filly prance to the roar of a crowd at the starting-gate. For another second she held her stance, and then she turned tail and ran, followed by the calf. No other member of the herd was within the field of the telescope, but now as I swept the hill-side I saw them all on the move. They were making for the high ground, and all bore the signs of panic.

" They've bolted," I said.

The man on the rock raised himself to his elbow. Yet he didn't bother to reach for his glasses. Instead, he touched his pipe with a gesture, and puffed a cloud of smoke from his lips which went drifting down-wind after the herd.

. . . .

We saw them on the high ground—a score at the head of a corrie where the slope eased into a shallow step below the crest of the hill. Through the telescope, the shades of their hides were well marked against the dark background. There was one big fellow, darker than the rest, who lay in the centre of the group—and with a head on him which he doubtless knew merited precautions.

It was an easy stalk during its early stages. At the outset, I could see through the glasses a fault in the mountain-side which started several hundred feet below the herd as an open scar, and ran upwards to a diminishing but darker streak on the mountain three hundred yards from the nearest beast. Thereafter, the matter might be in the lap of the gods, but as there were boulders breaking through the heather, and the heather itself had that patchy look which often denotes depth, there was little reason for pessimism. More-over, the deer were settled, most of them lying down in the bright, warm sun.

We worked our way up-wind along the steep slope,

made use of a shallow corrie where we lost two or three hundred feet of unwanted height, and so came along the face of the mountain into the depression of the scar. We had been well screened, and in little more than half an hour we found ourselves lying in a bed of heather at eye-level with the herd and not more than two hundred and fifty yards away. The intervening ground lay deep in patches of the same old growth, with here and there a boulder to assist the final approach.

The stag we coveted was still lying down, half-hidden in the heather. For the moment, we were content with him as he was, and happy enough, too, in the sight of another young stag which lay close to him—no doubt playing the role of watcher. There were some hinds in the background, and others up the slope—but we had hopes that these would not worry us. The real problem was an isolated beast well forward of the herd, and between us and our quarry. He was on his feet, head towards us, and grazing in a desultory way in a patch of grass. From where we lay, and on the projected line of our stalk, he must increase the range by an unwelcome thirty yards—a distance to be ill afforded. By the fall of the ground the shot would be long enough already. Unfortunately, as a target he had few attractions when compared with the darker-coloured beast on which we had set our hearts.

There was yet another choice higher up the slope. But he, too, was an inferior specimen, and apart from his lack of quality he could not be approached on our present line. We should need to make a retreat, and start a new stalk which would bring us down on him from above—a difficult enough venture in any case, for the ground was uncommonly bare, and there were hinds in profusion all round him.

So we decided to carry on, hoping to win at least another hundred yards. With luck, we might even shorten the range further by working down to the right, so avoiding by a wider margin the stag who was grazing.

Twenty minutes later, after wriggling forward with a degree of caution which would not have shamed a wild cat, we reached the limit to which it was safe to go. Immediately ahead was an almost imperceptible fold, with beyond it an open grass runner in full view of the stag. The other beast was perhaps a hundred and twenty yards away on our half-left, for we had broken down the slope to put him more on our beam. He was still on his feet and within a few yards of where we had seen him first.

The problem now was to get the big stag to his own feet. In the position where he lay he offered an indifferent target, for, although his head was visible, a hump of heather covered the whole of the lower part of his body—and there was no movement which we could make ourselves to improve the view. The range was about a hundred and thirty yards.

I thought of risking a shot at his head, but my companion knew my limitations with a rifle only too well, and he hissed me to silence. It was worth almost any risk, he whispered, to get the beast to his feet.

Anyone who has tried to do such a thing with hinds in the vicinity will appreciate the niceties of the situation. It was necessary to alarm him just sufficiently to get him to his legs, and yet not sufficiently to give warning to the hinds higher up the slope and only a little farther away. There was, moreover, the reaction of the nearer stag to be considered on our left. It is probably true that stags in good condition are only about half as prone to taking alarm as hinds, and considerably less than this when they are rutting. But both sexes will panic on scent, and we were left with the senses of either hearing or sight through which to give the warning which we now so desired.

The range suggested that the stag might stay where
he was if we showed ourselves, while the hinds,
somewhat farther away, might easily take fright.
They might, of course, pretend to go on grazing,
watching us all the time for another move. But it was
doubtful whether the risk of panicking the whole herd
was justified. Moreover, the stag on our left was only
a hundred-odd yards away, and at this distance a young
beast would have no doubt whatever of the nature of
the trouble ahead.

It looked a better risk to try sound. A very low
whistle must reach both stags, but if it was skilfully
pitched it should not reach the hinds. To this end, I
levelled the rifle and nodded to my companion.

It was a very low whistle indeed, and appeared
to have no effect on the quarry. The beast on our left
heard it, however, and raised his head. After standing
for a moment he took a pace or two towards us, and
stopped again. He was puzzled, and looked as though
he was prepared to investigate.

" Lend me your stick," whispered my companion.

I took one hand off the rifle and passed it back to
him. He clicked his own stick gently against mine,
and the big stag got to his feet as though he had received
an electric shock. For one brief second he stood outlined against the hill-side, while every other hind and
stag in the herd raised their heads. But the pause was
sufficient. As the panic seemed to spread from beast
to beast I pressed the trigger. The forest was short of
another fine beast.

.   .   .   .

It was a curious day, curious in its beginning and
its end. It accounted for a stag, an eagle's feather, and
a grouse's egg. Not an orthodox day by any means,
yet one which belongs to the forest and adds to a man's
friendship for it.

I had telephoned for a weather report soon after it was light—a modern facility which is not to be scorned on a day which will take a stalker beyond the 3000-foot contours.

"Warm, with the wind increasing to twenty-five knots, veering from the south-east to the south-west during the afternoon," said the distant voice. "Cloud ten-tenths at 800 feet, lifting to 1500 and breaking."

"Only fifteen hundred feet," I repeated.

"Yes," said the voice. "I don't think it will lift higher."

It was not promising. Yet I thought—more than thought, I was convinced—that a twenty-five-knot wind from the south-west would lift the cloud over the high-tops. It nearly always did, although if it came east of south the prophecy of the voice would come true. The south-east wind has the sea in it, and on these hills it condenses into drizzle before it is half-way up their sides.

I looked out of the window, saw the seventy-foot tree on the lawn disappearing into the mist, and across the meadow searched for the blue-grey smudge of the village church. Visibility was less than three hundred yards, and we were not a thousand feet above sea-level. Yet the wind which was blowing was a good wind. It was the one which brought the deer into this forest, and moreover it was a good stalking wind—all the way round through south into the south-west. Should the high-tops clear it might be a wonderful day.

So I rang up my host four miles further up the glen, where he lived in the last substantial house, and gave him my report.

"We'll risk it," he said.

Three hours later we reached the summit of a 2000-foot dome which lay curiously isolated at the bottom of the main glen. Between times, as the mist had swirled and billowed about us five miles away in the lower valley, we had set up a target and sighted the rifle. Now the day was before us, and we looked close under the roof of the clouds into the heart of the forest. It was the view enjoyed by the pilot who flies immediately under the overcast—of inverted domes, trailing curtains, and sudden windows, but with always a sight of the earth immediately below.

My host, expert stalker in his own forest, threw a handful of the coarse round grass of the hill-top into the air and watched it drift.

" Still south-east," he commented.

But if the wind blew from the old quarter, the base of the clouds was higher, much higher. Indeed, more than half that part of the forest which we hoped to stalk lay clear before us. We were looking directly up a magnificent glen, half a mile wide at its base, narrowing as it rose, until in the distance it terminated in a steep-sided corrie, where it was swallowed by the mist. Its entrance lay almost immediately below us, sweeping to the south, where its western rampart ended in an abrupt fall like the tip of a man's nose. Here it was joined by another glen and its burn, the combined streams flowing past the foot of our watch-tower, and so southward into the fringes of the forest by the way we had climbed.

It was the corrie at the head of the glen in which we were specially interested. The way ran straight in a level top for nearly five miles, ultimately joining a barrier wall which blocked off the end of the valley at a height of over 3000 feet. On the lower slopes of the wall were two mighty ravines, each of which might hold deer, but each capable of inspection from the high-top without the weariness of making the precipitous descent. The opposite wall was less spectacular, but as it subsequently turned out much more productive. It, too, climbed to the great barrier at the head of the valley, but its smooth back came down in a gentle descent to the junction of the glens at our feet.

In the ground between these two walls we pinned
our hopes. As we sat on the mountain-top we could
see perhaps three miles into the gloomy recess, leaving
a further mile or so of the upper reaches, together with
the guardian ridge, still hidden in the mist. All we
could see looked empty to the naked eye—a dirty yellow
waste at its base, where brief marshes gathered about
the burn, then blue-grey rock and the russet of heather,
with green runners where the sides rose on either hand.
But through our glasses it became peopled with deer.
I found a herd of perhaps thirty on the point of the
western rampart almost immediately beneath us, while
my companion picked out small parcels scattered up
the glen for as far as the edge of the mist. There were
too many of them for comfort, too many chances of
stumbling unawares on some isolated beast which
would put the whole forest on the move.

It was a fascinating moment to the casual stalker
unacquainted with the ground. I knew it all well
enough from the air, and I had walked its fringes.
But with the wind blowing into the glen in front of us
I knew it would be no simple problem. On the face
of it, it looked as though we might go down from our
mountain eyrie by the way we came, to break south into
the adjoining glen, and so over the dividing spur, where
we would be right above the larger herd which I had
seen first of all. In a straight line, across the airy spaces
of the valley, the distance was only a little over a mile.

" It won't work that way," said my companion.
" We must go round to the head of the glen along the
high-tops and come down on them by the rigging of
the western wall."

I tried to measure the distance with my eye. It
seemed a tremendous detour, for it meant walking the
whole length of the glen along the ridge which was still
lost in the mist, crossing the barrier rigging at its end,
and returning again down the opposite wall.

My host guessed some of my thoughts, for he looked at me with a rueful grin before he said: " It's the best part of three hours." Then he mitigated the sentence by saying : " We shall probably fall in with deer on the way." Yet I still wanted to argue, for if we went my way—to the left instead of to the right—we could cross the mouth of the glen well clear of the nearest herd and be under the cover of the western wall and into the adjoining glen without a deer having a chance to see us.

"We'll try it if you like," he said. " But I've attempted many stalks that way, under identical conditions, and I've always been winded."

It seemed that it was a trick of the south-easter to hug the valley floor at this point, and to carry the scent of the stalker round the corner farther than one would normally expect. It was true that one need never be within sight of anything in the main glen, nor within a thousand yards. Yet it remained a risky route.

So we set our faces to the high-tops, first descending a few hundred feet to a pass which joined our mountain to the main northern wall. In an hour we were tramping over level ground, with the pony cheerfully following in the rear. Up here the heather grew only a few inches high. It was like a rich pile carpet patterned with the curling fronds of ash-white lichen. Had not the mist kept down the visibility to thirty yards the prospect must have been magnificent. As it was, we were no more than ghosts to each other, while the outline of every hummock halted us in our tracks until we had established its identity. From the fresh droppings, and from the wisps of newly-cropped heather which were scattered at our feet, we knew that we must be surrounded by deer. At one place we came upon a freshly rubbed patch where a stag had ridded himself of a few strips of velvet. No wonder every shape in the mist sent our hearts into our mouths. Yet the only living things we saw were a covey of ptarmigan and a wandering ring-ouzel.

In another hour we were floundering in a moss-hag, making a hazardous way between its islands of solid ground—islands looking in the mist like the deserted altars of a primitive religion. They rose up from the red-black earth as though they had been chiselled with a peat-cutter's spade instead of owing their birth to the erosion of the mountain around them.

For a while we were compelled to cast this way and that for a way through. The weight of the pony was sinking its legs above the fetlocks, and for a moment we saw ourselves with a far more urgent problem than shooting a stag. Yet at last we came out on to the hard ground again and made on to the crest of the corrie itself. Here, standing on its lip, the cliff fell away at our feet into a cauldron of billowing silver. The day was degenerating into a disaster, for as we looked the mist steamed up over edge, to drive past on the wings of a wild wind like the plumes of a hundred chimneys, and with them came the first onslaught of the rain. We had hoped that by now the tops would be clear ; that we should be looking down from the top of the corrie into the long glen with the choice of half a dozen possible stalks. As it was, we had only this sight of the driving clouds, and the knowledge that in our passage along the high ground we had moved a score or more of unseen deer. If they had gone over the march into the great glen to the north, well and good, though we should have lost them for the day. If they had broken south into our own glen, they might have put its whole population on the move. Seeing nothing, and knowing nothing, we felt impotent.

There was little to be done save to work round on to the western wall, striking along its descending crest into the teeth of the wind, and hoping for a clearance at a lower level. After all, we had been promised only a ceiling of 1500 feet and at this moment we were at 3000. So down we went through the driving rain, until every rag on our bodies was whipped about our limbs in sodden stickiness. Twice we left the pony to descend the face of the wall itself in search of clear air, each time to struggle back without sight of anything but shadow forms of the rocks. It was strange that we never stumbled upon one of the many beasts which we had seen grazing on the slopes in the morning. Had my companion not possessed an almost supernatural bump of locality we might have believed that our footsteps had strayed. Yet once a green runner on which a stag had been standing was pointed out to me, and a few minutes later a blue-grey rock beside which another had been lying—all this in visibility of a few dozen paces. The same unerring sense led us back on each occasion to the pony and its patient gillie on the crest of the ridge.

It was now four hours since we had left our spy-top, and as we abandoned the pony for a third time, and yet another descent into the glen, we decided that if we failed to sight the valley floor we would quit the forest and hope for better days. No doubt the mountain gods heard the threat, and repented ; for as we went far down the hill-side a curtain was momentarily drawn aside and there beneath us was the burn and the hard wire grass and the glacial boulders with which the glen was strewn. In that instant, too, we saw on a steep slope about three hundred yards away the rigid forms of standing deer—ghosts of a moment, before the curtain was drawn again, and we were left wondering whether we had really seen them.

Then began a game of hide-and-seek. It was not stalking in the accepted sense of the word, but it was sufficient of a change to be exciting and to banish the weariness of the long hours behind us. As we crept forward the curtain was again swung aside, to reveal the deer in full view on a hill-side barren of cover, so that unless the mists closed we were in a parlous position. But, as I have suggested, the gods had relented, and after a few seconds the curtain was again drawn over the wild scene. This time we scrambled fiercely up the slope into safety, and working round began to make a cautious descent from above. In the brief interlude of clear air my host had already noted the only possible line of approach- -as nice a tribute to the speed of his judgement as a fellow-stalker could wish.

Yet the game was still no better than blindman's-buff. In a little while, sitting back on our haunches in a bed of watery heather, peering into the shapeless outlines thirty yards away, my host expressed the opinion that the deer were within fifty yards. It was a ridiculous position and it was only possible to wait for another clearance. It didn't come—not within the span of our dwindling patience—and we decided to move on, a foot at a time. So we came to the edge of a little crest, and behind it we paused to take counsel.

" Creep up and look over," whispered my companion. " Have the rifle ready."

Neither of us was prepared for the result. As we slithered to the crest on our bellies, and raised anxious heads above the top of the heather, we all but fell into the midst of the deer. I found myself eye to eye with a young stag, the astonishment written as clearly in his eyes as it must have been in mine. My companion subsequently claimed that he was so close to a hind that a running jump down the slope would have landed him astride her back. Other shadowy forms stood within twenty yards, every one of them with a pair of luminous brown eyes turned our way.

The matter became a question of whose reaction was the quickest. As far as I was concerned there was

L

never any doubt about it. Long before the rifle was at my shoulder, or even the safety catch slammed down, the rump of the nearest stag was presented for my approval. Nor do I believe that an ordinary man is capable of shooting so noble a beast in the backside at a range of fifteen yards. At twenty-five yards the affair might have seemed possible—but at just that distance the beast was swallowed by the mist. Instead of a bullet sent after him, he was pursued by echoing gusts of laughter.

The farce was ended. The sportsmen were satisfied. They were now only too anxious to be quit of the hill, relishing the moment with grim amusement and wondering, after all, if they had been a little quicker a murder might not have been committed with the knife ! They had both heard stories of men so accomplished that a stalk had ended with a quick knife-thrust between the ribs—a nice story to tell after the port had been round.

It was in the midst of such thoughts, as we clumped down the hill, that the sport of the day began in earnest. First came another rift in the clouds, and with it a speck which grew out of the sky to reveal itself as a golden eagle soaring the slope wind. It held a steady course on rigid wings, growing from a ghost in the mist to a hard black outline which sailed directly over our heads. My companion raised his rifle, steadied it for an instant as he lay on his back, and fired. Instantly after the report I saw the pinions of a wing open and shut, as though a bullet had passed between them. The eagle faltered, lost height as it slipped sideways down the path of the wind, recovered, and under full power turned across the valley towards the opposite mountain. In a moment it was gathered into the hanging bosom of a cloud which drifted between us, while from the place where it had been a feather fluttered down in a gentle see-saw. I went to recover it and, as I picked it up from the heather, I saw beneath the place where it had lain a deserted nest. In it were the shells of five grouse eggs which had been successfully hatched, and a sixth egg, whole and perfect. The egg and the feather went into my pockets, the one to be added to a little girl's collection, the other to be tied into a new kind of salmon fly. I had never seen a salmon fly dressed with an eagle's feather—but I saw one now in my mind's eye. It had a body of royal purple overwound with gold ribbing and a topping of golden pheasant poised above the wing.

I returned elated to my companion, and we continued our way down the slope where it fell steeply in its final plunge to the valley floor. Now we were at last below the ceiling of swirling vapour, and immediately ahead was the junction of the two burns where the hill ended like a man's nose. Down there, by a ruined shieling, we had arranged to meet the pony. It must have been well on its way, for the path down the opposite slope of the nose was more gentle and the ground easy. He would come this way, for it was clear of the path of our last abortive stalk.

With the day finally done, we heard from our right, suddenly, dramatically, the sharp ting of a wire fence struck by a hoof. It was the sheep fence, and it came out of the silence of the hills like a cymbal sounded unexpectedly in the night. My host, who was still carrying the rifle, ran forward, reached the skyline which formed the tip of the nose within twenty yards, and dropped to one knee. I was close behind him, and was in time to see, streaming across the gentle slope towards the burn, a herd of deer in full flight. The rearmost hind was caught in the retina of my eye as though by a camera, poised in mid-air above the top wire of the fence. The remainder were strung out fifty yards ahead, two fine stags in the centre of the fleeing column, several smaller beasts in the van, and clear in the lead a young stag moving with the speed and grace of the wind. They were crossing from right to left, almost certainly put up by the pony.

The chance which came now was not one which I would have dared to take myself so late in the day—or indeed at any time. Although the nearest beast was no more than sixty yards away, it was too well covered by running hinds to make a shot possible. For a fraction of a second, I saw the shoulder of a good stag clear of the ruck, yet a bullet which struck it must have also wounded the beast beyond. The only chance was the young stag in front. He was moving fast, and was at least a hundred yards away. Yet I saw my companion pick it, level the rifle as he rested on one knee, and shoot. The beast stumbled, regained its footing, and went on as fast as ever, reaching the burn twenty yards ahead of the next behind it. Then for a while it was lost as the milling crowd reached the water and began to cross it. The leaders went over and the column began to string out again on the steep slope of the opposite face. But the wounded stag was still indistinguishable. Nor was there to be much chance to identify it, for the mist still hung down to within three hundred feet of the valley floor, cutting a clean grey line across the dark mountain-side. In half a minute or so, all but the last of the deer were swallowed.

Then we saw a stag which appeared to be moving slower than the rest. He even stopped for a moment, and gave us a chance to get the glasses on to him. He was fully four hundred yards away, but he had the look of our own beast, though as he turned for the mist again he seemed strong enough. As he moved, the cloud came down to meet him, and making the best of the opportunity ourselves we raced down the hill for another hundred yards. Then once more the cloud lifted and forced us to lie still. We scanned the hill-side with our glasses, and picked him up. He stood

in a patch of heather, head held high and turned
our way, and as we looked he began to walk slowly
along the face of the slope. In that moment we saw
ourselves following him up that bitter hill, the night
advancing, and our feet more weary than we could
believe.

But the gods smiled at last. The stag stopped
again, half-turned towards us, and my companion
raised his rifle. The range was at least three hundred
yards, and the angle most awkward. Save for the flat
face of the head there was little to be seen but the rear
quarters. I held my breath and offered up a silent
prayer. There was an instant's pause, and then the
report of the rifle. I was watching the stag, and the
result of the shot was dramatic. The beast collapsed
as though all four legs had been knocked from under
him. As he crumpled, his body turned over before
it reached the ground, and came gyrating down the
slope in deathly abandon.

When we followed across the burn and up the hill
we saw that the bullet had taken him between the eyes
and had come out at the back of the head. It was a
remarkable shot. Nor was the first attempt much
inferior, for we found a wound high up in the gralloch,
perhaps six inches too far back to be immediately fatal,
and yet correct for elevation. On a running stag it had
been no mean performance.

" A fluke," said my companion.

But I knew better, for he was not a man who would
take a stag wantonly—without more than a good chance
of grassing it.

As the pony reached the burn we dragged the
carcass down the last of the precipitous slope, and were
far advanced in the final rites before the saddle was
ready. Within a few minutes, head and forelegs
trussed, the carcass was flung across the pony's back
and we turned our faces down the long glen in the

direction of civilisation. The last memory we took
away with us was the sight of a pair of ravens swinging
impatiently across the face of the mountain, speeding
us on our way, so that the gralloch could be theirs
before night fell.

CHAPTER XI

WITH A RIFLE

IT was to be a big day. A dozen beaters had already assembled and were now jostling each other into the limited interior of a shooting brake. As each new body pushed its way inside, the springs sank visibly lower. On the roof of the brake somebody had thrown a bundle of white flags tied with a piece of rope, the first jolt of the road destined to fling it off. Near by stood the host, in close converse with the keeper, heads bent together like distinguished politicians at a time of crisis. In the background a servant was stowing picnic-baskets into a lorry, while another was calling for help with a case of clinking bottles. A gun left standing against the house wall was brushed by the trailing coat of a guest, and slithered with a clatter to the gravel. Its owner leapt to save it, like a mother snatching her child from beneath the wheels of a bus. He was too late, swore rudely, and was mollified by apologies which quickly turned into an exchange of compliments. The gun was undamaged.

A familiar scene—and one which the boy in the cloth cap and tight breeches had come to dislike. Somehow he disliked it more than ever this morning. One of the guests, a man with a sloppy body and a drooping moustache, had been patronising him, looking over his head while he talked. The boy disliked the man quite intensely. In fact he disliked everyone gathered round the house except his father and the keeper. His father was a beneficent being of whom he was very proud. The keeper was as good as an uncle, and a real friend. It was he who had taken him out all through the previous year, shooting up the long valley,

and teaching him many more things besides the
handling of a gun.

The boy summoned up his courage and approached
his father. It was an anxious moment, because he knew
suddenly that he was going to resolve all his doubts
in a single, shattering announcement. He tried to keep
his voice level.

" I'm not going out with you to-day—that is, if
you don't mind." The rider was an afterthought which
he was unable to check.

He saw his father's face cloud with anxiety, saw
his eyes search swiftly among the crowd until they came
to rest on his mother, where she stood on the steps
leading down from the porch.

" Feeling rotten ? "

He shook his head. His father didn't understand,
and he himself couldn't explain. It was a psychological
nicety beyond his powers of analysis. How was he to
tell him that the hurricanes of grouse which he knew
were destined to fly over his butt could be no palliative
to the disquiet of a day spent among uncongenial elders
—and, far more important, that he thought the quality
of the sport was so poor that he would sooner be almost
anywhere else ? Impossible ! Not even to his secret
self could he admit the thing that lay behind it—that
his childhood dreams were still real, that he still saw
himself in the rôle of his story-book heroes who were
great hunters, heroes who never once in the long train
of books which lined the deserted nursery shelf shot
grouse from a butt. They were making an automaton
of him, an instrument for killing fast-moving birds in
which he had no interest. He had recently overheard
the booming voice of one of his father's friends say that
he had never seen a seventeen-year-old shaping better.
Well it was a shape he didn't like, and the flattery went
by like a cold wind.

" All right," said his father in a puzzled way, " you

stay behind." As he spoke, the boy saw his father's eyes stray through an opening in the trees to where the swift figure of another boy was running with a tennis racquet. A light of understanding spread across his face.

The boy watched from the sanctuary of a window the last of the guests depart. Then he went swiftly to the gun-room, from where he took a light rifle, and then to his father's desk—to the middle drawer, where there was a tight, cardboard box of ammunition. With these he left the house by the back door, darted down the path through the trees, passed the empty kennels, the stables, and the gate leading into the long valley. He took the track through the high ferns, leaving it to wade the stream and come to the shepherd's cottage where the swamp began. It was here that the duck lived and where the experience of the previous year taught him that sport began. If there were no duck there were rabbits, and he'd seen woodcock in swift, straight flight to the east after dark, and snipe, and even partridges in the wild weather—some of these things only in the dead of winter, but all of them present in his memory on this hot September day. He stood at the gate of the world he wanted.

In another hour he was sitting on a tuft of heather far beyond the bog, the rifle resting easily across his knees. This was the moment for which he had staked his inarticulate beliefs. It was new and exciting, and beautifully orchestrated by the tinkling burn and the wind and the far call of the birds. As he waited, he knew that something would happen.

The call of a cock grouse caused him to look up. It came from the hill-side, and ranging the heather with his eyes he saw the dark wings against a lighter background. They were floating towards him as though preordained to sail down the hill this way—to pitch into another clump of heather a hundred yards away across the stream.

He began to stalk the owner of the wings, sliding forward on his stomach and pushing the rifle ahead of him. Now and again he could see the grouse strutting through the heather, moving a little at a time in the direction of the water. Once, while he was resting, because he feared to move too fast, he heard the hen bird call, and a moment afterwards saw another black outline sliding down the purple canopy of the hill. She too pitched into the opposite heather, but a dozen yards away from her companion. It was lucky, thought the boy, that he was not moving at the time.

So he came to within seventy yards, and felt he dare go no farther. Presently the cock bird came on to a little bare patch of ground with a grey stone breaking out of the heather for a background. Its head was raised as though it were listening, and its body was held rigid, as an ordinary man might hold himself when brought to an alert. The boy lifted the rifle and perched the bird securely on the tip of the foresight. He steadied, and squeezed the trigger.

The rifle made little sound—just a sharp crack like the snapping of a bough. But it was followed instantly by the decisive plunk of a bullet hitting soft flesh and feathers. The boy saw that the grouse was dead.

It was a long time ago, so long that the sunshine of the afternoon percolates only thinly through the filter of the years. Yet it still lights every incident, still washes the rock of conviction which was formed on this September day. In the years which have gone, many a temptation has disintegrated against this rock—the temptation of the line of beaters driving the birds before it like spray, the temptation of the coverts when the pheasants were tumbling from the height of church steeples, the temptation of the hail of partridges driven across the stubbles ; all those things which owe their existence and success to organisation and co-operative effort. But they have not always been resisted when the opportunity offered. They have merely not been admitted into the place which is reserved for a lover. The boy is a man. He survived his reluctance to go out with his father's friends grouse-driving, because he was allowed to discover for himself the things which were in its background, the life and movement of the moor, stream, covert, and bog. This was knowledge which could only be learned alone, sitting on a rock, creeping through the heather, merging with the shadows of the trees, scanning the field from a hedge-bottom. Once it had been acquired, however slightly and for-getfully, it no longer seemed artificial and distasteful to take part in big days attended by many people.

It was the sort of lesson which was well learnt with a rifle. With a shot-gun, it was too easy to learn care-lessly, knowing that the game could be brought down in flight. It was fun to walk up the valley at any time, but the discovery of the little Martini in a corner of the gun-room made of the valley something which it had never been before. Its failures—and there were many —each added their lesson, and it wasn't long before the ability to shoot straight was rated at a new value. It is a value which is not understood by many an older man—by many a deer-stalker who believes that he owes his success in the forest to his accuracy in shooting. Only let him go out on to the moor and try to kill a brace of grouse before lunch, and subtleties deeper than marksmanship will be revealed to him.

It is not long since I was leaning over the bar of a Highland inn, listening to the talk of shepherds, sipping brown ale, and thinking to myself in between times how wonderfully well I proposed to sleep that night. The wind on the moor had been wild, and I had walked far for very little reward. Now in the light of an oil-lamp everything seemed to be misted—pleasantly misted with soft light through my tired eyes. It was little more than chance that I caught a remark of one of the shepherds—that there were duck on the loch. Duck, stalked with a rifle, were something which had raised my spirits to a giddy pinnacle of elation—whenever the stalk had been successful—and after an almost fruitless day with a shot-gun the words of the shepherd inspired fresh hope and energy.

It was a difficult loch. I knew it well, and in sober moments I might have admitted that it was impossible to stalk. But it was the more interesting for this reason, and the fact that the birds might be shot easily at the morning flight did not detract from the more difficult task of bagging a single specimen in full daylight with a rifle.

The following morning I came over the hill which sloped down on its farther side to the sheet of sheltered water. At a distance of half a mile I saw the gently curving bays, the long reeds at its head, the square, sandy shore of its southern end, and the trickle which drained from its shallows to form a channel through the heather and the beginnings of a burn. Far up the shore, at the narrow neck where the water merged into the reeds and the reeds merged into the moorland valley, I saw the duck. There were perhaps two hundred of them, a dark, weed-like patch covering the upper end of the loch. The majority were mallard, but among them were golden-eye, or possibly tufted duck. The distance was too great to be sure, even with the help of glasses.

I carried a ·22 rifle fitted with a telescopic sight of small magnification. With the ammunition I was using it was an effective weapon up to three hundred yards— a fact of purely academic interest, for I had never succeeded in killing anything at more than half such a range.

The problem at first sight looked insoluble. There
was not a scrap of cover within a mile of the loch, except
for a single tree which sprang out of a patch of grass
within thirty yards of the edge of the water. Every-
where the bare hill-sides sloped down to the margin,
only heather, with occasional green runners, clothing
their flanks. At the shallow, sandy end the slopes
shrank back a little to offer a slight depression through
which the outflow escaped. But it was at the opposite
end to the duck.

I had, however, the stalker's attitude of mind that
morning. It was nurtured by a warm sun and a windless
sky, so that the prospect of lying full length on the hill-
top, and remaining there for an hour or more while a
possible approach was devised, in no way made me
impatient. I think that even a duck sitting on an open
sheet of water needs to respect this attitude. However
poor a shot a man may be, he is a deadly enemy if he has
forgotten the Latin tag of *tempus fugit*, for he is liable
to come surprisingly close to the creatures he hunts.
Like the long-delayed darkness of a summer night,
the quarry may find himself overtaken before the threat
has become apparent.

So it was that a possibility formed itself in my mind.
It revolved about the single tree by the side of the water.
If it were possible to place its network of branches
between myself and the duck, it might not be difficult
to reach its base. The clothes I was wearing blended
with the old browns of the dead heather-blossom,
and, once a point on the hill-side some three hundred
yards below was reached, the tree would begin to
play its part. If it were possible to reach its shelter,
the nearest duck would be about a hundred yards
away.

The long journey was begun, but not before my
piece of camouflage netting had been draped over my
hat. I kept to the dividing line of the heather and the

lighter patches of grass, for at such a boundary it has always seemed that movement is more difficult to detect. In a quarter of an hour a place was reached where the heather had been burnt, the strip running downhill in the general direction of the tree. Movement along it was made cautiously, about ten paces at a time, followed by a pause of two or three minutes. It was in no way tedious, for I stood upright and made no conscious effort to hide. Experience suggests strongly that the sight of a man standing absolutely still, although in full view, is less dangerous than rapid movement in which only a small part of him is visible, and less dangerous still than his scent carried on a following wind.

I was about a hundred yards from the tree, with its branches nicely covering a proportion of the resting duck, when far up the opposite hill-side I caught the glint of a movement. With the help of the glasses, I realised that what I had seen was the white front of the shepherd's dog. Behind him was the shepherd himself, moving along the face of the hill. On his present track he would be carried past the southern end of the loch, clearing it by perhaps a quarter of a mile. Would the duck rise ?

There was nothing to do but to lie and wait. I saw him reach a point opposite when he was no more than four hundred yards from the nearest birds. He had dropped down the hill-side, and if he continued on his present track I could count my mission finished. At this moment, I saw a white feather on the water as the birds rose, a flight of a score perhaps, followed in another moment by a dozen more. The smaller heads of the golden-eye began drifting in towards my own bank, and the probability was that they, at least, would not rise. The mallard circled but, with a wave of hope, I saw that they were not climbing. In less than another minute it was clear that they had no intention of leaving their sanctuary if they could help it. At this moment the shepherd altered course. There was evidently a track running parallel to the length of the loch, and he was now being carried away from the duck which still remained on the water. Slowly, infinitely slowly it seemed, he moved across the face of the hill. The mallard continued to circle, but a portion of the first flight had already made a turn over the bay in the farthest corner, close to the reeds. Here they pitched with a smother of foam which I could hear even at this distance. They would be not more than ninety yards from the tree.

The danger passed. Half a dozen mallard alone had climbed into the blue sky, and I saw the last of them flying between the shoulders of the two northern peaks on their way deeper into the mountains. But it was half an hour before I moved again. The birds would be restless, and suspicious.

Within fifty yards of the tree I dropped to my stomach and wriggled down the edge of a grass runner which led me up to the base of the trunk itself. Only thirty yards away the small ripple sucked at the peat of the overhanging bank, and twenty yards out the nearest golden-eye bobbed on the surface. There were at least another score scattered across the loch beyond them, with a much larger bunch close in to the reeds of the farther bank. There was an opportunity now to bag a bird. The range was not excessive and the light was perfect. But I wanted a mallard rather than a golden-eye (there were no tufted duck on the loch as I had originally supposed). It was an ambition which seemed reasonable, for I knew that they were concentrated in the bay on my left which was hidden by the gentle shoulder of ground which reached out from the foot of the hill to form the intervening point. The only question was whether the golden-eye would take to the wing if I moved.

It seemed a risk worth accepting, and so it was that I continued the crawl on my stomach, only this time I moved at no more than a yard at a time. Out of one eye I kept a watch on the nearest duck. They saw me clearly enough but, as I had hoped, their only reaction was to swim slowly towards the centre of the loch. I knew I was safe. In ten minutes I was immediately beneath the low crest which hid my vision of the bay. Within a second or two I should know the quality of my chances. I raised my head. I looked down into the bay, and there sixty yards away were such a collection of mallard as would bring tears of happiness into the eyes of a punt gunner. For a single unworthy moment I wished that I had such a gun. The rifle could never do justice to such a target.

Even now, haste might ruin the chances. So it was a very slow movement which slid a cartridge into the breech. Three other shells were laid beside me on the grass, for it seemed possible that more than one shot might be had. After firing the first shot it would be a matter of reloading regardless of noise or disturbance. There would be disturbance enough on the water.

With the telescopic sight, and a trajectory which was very flat, the shot was an easy one. I picked a drake, and fired at the centre of its body on the water-line. The bird never moved, and for a second I thought I had missed it. The ensuing commotion among the duck was sensational ; but, amongst it, I saw that there were two or three close against the reeds, a hundred yards away, which hadn't moved. I had just time to line up the rifle once again and fire. In the mass of whirling wings above the bay the result was not observed. But the bird at which I had fired was miraculously stationary, and it had occupied the hair-lines of the sight in a manner which gave me every hope.

In a minute it was all over. Hard against the reeds was the second body for which I had been looking.

Drifting gently towards me was another—the drake at which I had first fired. The surface of the loch was empty save for a few bobbing feathers and these two victims. I collected them, a drake and a duck in their full winter plumage, and bore them in triumph across the hill. Never before had I killed two birds with a rifle as a result of a single stalk.

That night I came again into the bar of the inn, and again the shepherds were gathered within the circle of yellow light.

" I saw the duck again," said the man who had spoken the night before.

" So did I," I said.

" Somebody disturbed them," he added. " They were gone when I came over the hill to-night."

" They'll be back," said another shepherd.

" Yes—they'll be back," he echoed.

The innkeeper leaned over the bar and spoke to me. " You might get a shot at them, sir, in the morning before it's light."

" I might," I said.

I don't think that a stalk such as this is a good one to attempt without previous experience. Although there was nothing difficult about it, the acquisition of the right state of mind is sometimes impossible, and without it, one might as well stay at home. An average quality of field sense is sufficient, but to apply it by movements which are more in keeping with a tortoise's, and often conducted in an attitude of extreme dis-comfort, usually leads to a breakdown in the stalker's patience. Anyone who has tried a long crawl through the pointed roots and the residue of burnt heather, for instance, will understand the physical reluctance to prolong the exercise to the point necessary for success. A few failures—and I've had my share of them—are likely to persuade a man that a rifle is of no use to him,

M

and in this he will lose one of the delights of a most entertaining aspect of sport.

Duck are easy enough when they are sitting on a well-screened pond. An up-wind approach, made without hurry, will more often than not give the chance of a shot. They can, similarly, be flighted at dawn and dusk, but to my mind the sport at such times is better with a scatter gun. I have never liked the idea of killing a sitting bird at the moment it believes it has achieved the sanctuary of the water. In full daylight, with the odds more equally balanced, I know of no more pleasant way of spending an hour or two.

Grouse, too, are hardly the right game for a beginner, although my first stalk turned out so successfully. Grouse are birds which repay watching, for they have their special habits like other game. Of all birds, the casual shooter knows least about them, and as a consequence he is unlikely to be immediately successful.

The traditional game for a ·22 is, of course, the humble rabbit, probably because the skill demanded for success is not high. The ability to lie quietly under the cover of a bush while the bunnies come out of a wood to feed is, after all, a modest achievement. To sit patiently outside a warren is sport on the same level. On the other hand, the killing of a rabbit at anything over fifty yards demands fair marksmanship, particularly if the rabbit is within a few yards of its burrow. Unless it is hit in the head it will probably reach the sanctuary of its hole, to die a lingering death. It is quite possible to drill a hole through it, almost anywhere, and to see it struggle back to its home. It is not a sight which adds distinction to the sport. On the other hand, the head of a rabbit fifty yards away is a sufficiently large target to make reasonably certain of a kill. At a hundred yards there must be an element of doubt about it, for not every rifle commands the requisite accuracy. Nor, as far I am concerned, could I guarantee to shoot straight at this range.

Accuracy with a miniature rifle is measured to fine limits by those who know about these things. I once boasted to a friend that I could hit a penny with ten consecutive shots at thirty yards. He smiled in a kindly way and asked whether I thought this was good shooting. I said that it wasn't bad, and probably better than he could do. For answer, he offered to hit a threepenny-bit as many times at the same range. I don't know whether he could have substantiated his threat, but he pointed out that even the duffers who paid their entrance money at Bisley were expected to fire a dozen shots for only one hole in the target at short range. If I could command such skill—and it is less rare than many suppose — my treatment of this chapter might well have been different. In the meantime, I recommend rabbits at not more than fifty yards for a beginner.

There is, undoubtedly, a higher degree of sport in stalking hares. It is an art which has its special devotees, and on the few occasions on which I have gone out after them the hares have usually had the better of me. I have found them unusually difficult to spot when lying in their scrapes, and have been compelled to rely on putting up my quarry and then standing still, hoping for it to stop and give me a chance. I am sure that this is not the right way to seek for the sport. I have had more success with partridges, which really ought to be more difficult. While in the first case it has always been a matter of luck with me, I have been able to conduct a genuine stalk in the second. The birds can either be shot when they come out to feed on the stubbles in the late afternoon—a practice which is to be deplored if the ground is a part of a normal shoot— or stalked on the basis of one's local knowledge. In the latter instance, it is the shallow hollow in the field which, approached up-wind, reveals the unsuspecting

covey. The range is usually short, and the pleasure
of it is contained in the rectitude of one's good judgement that this particular place should be sheltering the
birds at this particular time. I have stalked pigeons
under the same rules. The oasis of wind-levelled grain,
the stack-yard, and the open stubble—each of them
profitable places in their own time, and all of them
demanding a modicum of field sense.

I can imagine no better way of founding a love of
sport in a boy than by giving him a rifle, and sending
him off to hunt, and thereby all unconsciously to learn
the ways of wild creatures. Whether he will shoot
anything besides the things he aims at is a risk which
must be underwritten by careful training. In my own
case, I might well have found myself detained during
His Majesty's pleasure had I not enjoyed a generous
share of luck. But then I started under my own
auspices, urged on by a sense of injury through having
to stay back at my " prep " school during the holidays
as a result of mumps—contracted on the last day of the
term. Two other boys and myself, both of them Irish,
" borrowed " the rifles from the school's miniature
range, and commenced operations from the sickroom
window. The first target was the door-handle of the
School House, which was only some fifty yards away,
and if the headmaster cares to look closely at the door
to-day he will see the marks which are now nearly
thirty years old. But the target soon proved unexciting,
and we turned our marksmanship on to the panes of
glass in the street lamps of the residential road beyond
the gates. We shot out every one of them within two
hundred and fifty yards, reserving our fire only until
the unwitting pedestrians had taken a pace out of the
immediate line. The sport continued, with variations,
until a gardener who had been mowing one of the
suburban lawns presented himself at the school, hat
in hand. The hat had a hole in it.

This incident had a sobering effect, and since that time I have never forgotten that a rifle is lethal at a very long range. It should not, normally, be necessary to make a hole in somebody's hat to realise this, and, as I personally believe that the average boy is no greater fool than the average man, I should never forbid the joys of a rifle on the grounds of its danger. So long as we admit the mixed blessings of such diverse things as motor-cycles, atomic bombs, and pretty girls we can surely give a boy his head with a steel tube, a piece of lead, and a few grains of powder. It will certainly teach him more in a few weeks than as many years spent in the wake of his elders with a shot-gun.

NOTES

Geese, Duck, Red Deer

The following notes are not intended as an experiment in literary transmutation. Nobody could turn this book into a text-book. But many varieties of wildfowl and game have appeared in its pages, and in most instances without information concerning them, outside the immediate demands of the narrative. A brief, factual background of the lives and habits of a few of them may, therefore, fill a gap for those readers who do not happen to be acquainted with them. I have often read a book whose author has assumed a knowledge on my part which I didn't possess, and I would have been grateful for a chapter of references. This is what I have tried to provide here.

Geese

Far to the north, among the Arctic islands, in Iceland, Scandinavia, and Siberia, the majority of the geese which we know here in the winter have their beginnings. In the loneliness of unpeopled places, on floating islands of rotting vegetation, among the reeds, on the open tundra, in grassy tussocks, in thickets of dwarf willow and birch, on ledges and terraces in the face of cliffs, on islets in great rivers, on mountain-sides to the limits of the snow-line, in all the places of desolation left to northern Europe, the various species, mated for life, lay their eggs and bring up their young. During the brief Arctic summer, when the air has the clarity of the finest crystal, and the sun heats the rocks so that they could scarcely be touched by the hand, all the lessons which a wild bird must know if it is to survive are learned. By September the sun is swinging low between the horizons, the vegetation which bursts suddenly and generously out of the earth is withering, the first tinkling ice fringes the margin of the lakes, and the geese from the steppes of Siberia to the rocky coasts of Greenland know that the days in their homeland are numbered.

They migrate. They fly south, because winter in the Arctic has no more attraction for them than our own winter for the swallows. They are a part of the mass exodus which is taking place all over the northern hemisphere—the universal quest for warmth, and with it the quest for good food. The urge, if not the means, is common to most creatures which have their being on the earth.

In spring, when the midday sun is smearing a watery glint on the northern glaciers, and the first spring flowers are pushing their way through the newly softened top-soil of the lowest levels, the visitors go home. By the beginning of May the desolation is no longer so complete.

Of the dozen or so species which are comparatively common in Europe, six are well-known visitors to the British Isles. The rest are either so rare, or so infrequent in their arrivals, that a wildfowler may live his life without seeing them. The Red-breasted Goose, for instance, was last seen in the British Isles in February 1941, while previous to this a bird was recorded at Milford Haven in 1935. The Greater Snow Goose has been identified only a dozen times in the last hundred years, and the common Snow Goose perhaps a score of times in the oldest living memory.

The geese which make the sea-crossing regularly to our islands are the greylags, the pink-feet, the whitefronted and the bean geese, known collectively as the Grey Geese, and the brent and the barnacle, belonging to the genus of Black Geese. Of the six, only the grey-

lag breeds in the British Isles, and even here, there is
evidence pointing to its decline. Two hundred years
ago it was nesting regularly in Yorkshire and Cambridge,
and a hundred and fifty years ago in Lincolnshire and
Norfolk. To-day its nest is rare anywhere outside
northern Scotland.

It is the finest as well as the biggest of the wild geese
—an opinion admittedly influenced because I happen
to have shot and eaten it most often. Its weight is in
the neighbourhood of eight pounds, or a couple of
pounds heavier than the more widely distributed pink-
feet. The wildfowlers of eastern Scotland know it well,
particularly on the Tay and on the lowlands of Perth-
shire. Elsewhere, except on the Solway marshes, it is
comparatively scarce. It is easily recognisable by its
ash-brown plumage, orange beak with white nail, pale
pink feet, and large head. At first sight it bears a strong
resemblance (in common with the other grey geese) to
the domesticated variety and its voice seems to be
identical. It is only when one notices its walk that
one realises that the waddle is absent. During the
moult, which is a flightless period spent in the most
secluded marshes, it is said that it can cover the ground
at a run which would do credit to a cock pheasant.

In common with all grey geese, it usually feeds by
day, although when it is harried by gunners it is not
above changing its habits. At night, the normal practice
is to flight to the estuaries and the tide-washed sands
which can be regarded as sanctuary. In moonlight,
the day-feeding period is usually prolonged—or reversed—so that the wildfowler in his pit dug among the
sand dunes may have a long wait.

The principal precautions taken while feeding are
the choice of open ground difficult to approach without
being seen, and the apparent posting of sentries who,
unlike their human counterparts, never sleep on duty.
Who chooses the sentries on arrival at the feeding

ground is a mystery, but certain birds move, as though by common agreement, to the edge of the flock and, however tempting the dinner, keep their necks held high and their eyes open. When the sentry considers that her tour of duty is over, it is said that she often moves to the nearest bird and gives her a peck. I have actually seen this happen—although only once. The other bird then takes over, and there is no argument about it. This extraordinary discipline is one of the fascinating sidelights of a stalk.

I indicated in early chapters the type of food which the geese favour. It is not necessary to add much more, except to state the obvious—that the menu depends largely upon what is available. The greylag has a special partiality for oat stubbles, while the pink-feet prefer barley. But both like potatoes, young corn, and grass, and when an exceptionally hard winter drives, I doubt whether there is anything in a British field which will be refused.

In flight, the birds look rather clumsy and un-manœuvrable. It is a delusion, as anyone who has followed them in an aeroplane can testify. Steep turns, and a curious sort of side-slip, are standard evasive actions at which they are expert. From the ground, their rate of climb is by no means poor. I have waited at the edge of a field while the birds in its centre were put up by a friend from the opposite side, and have been astonished at the height they have gained in a short space. While flighting, they appear to favour any altitude up to fifteen hundred feet in calm weather, depending largely on how much they have been harried. When a battalion of our late gallant Allies were stationed on Buddon Ness the geese by-passed the area at a phenomenal altitude. They had discovered the lethal range of a sten gun to a nicety. In rough weather and more normal times they will often flight within shot.

During their journeys, passage is made in either vic or echelon formation. As a professional airman of several years' standing, I think less of their station-keeping than does the average naturalist, although it must be admitted that the distance between birds is maintained with an accuracy which would do credit to an air circus. I have noticed when ranging alongside a vic that the geese are stepped down in the best Service tradition, the leading bird occupying the highest altitude. The choice of the leader is no doubt a matter of wildfowl rank. Experienced sportsmen have suggested that the eldest bird assumes the privilege.

I think it likely that large flights are often preceded to a feeding ground by a scout. I have certainly noticed that a single bird or an odd pair have sometimes come in ahead of the main body, as though sent forward to make sure that the ground was clear. During the flight, the conversational efforts of the flock are remarkable, and (continuing Service parlance) one might suggest that their intercommunication procedure needs tightening up. They sound like a distant pack of hounds in full cry. On the ground, their gungling is more subdued.

What has been said of the greylag can be said in most parts of the pink-feet. They are, of course, a distinct species and even during their winter visitations rarely mix. While the greylag breeds essentially in Iceland, and is spread throughout Scandinavia to as far as northern Russia and down into Roumania, where it meets the Eastern race, the pink-feet breed only in the north-east corner of Greenland, Iceland, and Spits-bergen. And whereas the greylag favours for its nest the moorlands, the secluded marshes and the willow thickets, the pink-feet nest on ledges in the face of cliffs and among the rocks of the valleys—generally in colonies. But they both begin to arrive in this country at about the same time (at the end of September), and both leave again from February and onwards until April. Their favourite areas are also partially common. They abound from the Dornoch Firth to Norfolk, in the Solway, and the estuaries of the Ribble and the Severn. In the Tay area I have seen them within a few hundred yards of the greylags.

The illusion about pink-feet is contained in their name, for their feet are not so obviously pink as those of the greylag. They are, on the other hand, a very grey goose with a dark head and neck, and a small pink beak with a black base and nail.

The white-fronted goose, no doubt so called because of the extensive white patch on its face, is another widely distributed species, ranging from the Hebrides to the bogs of Ireland, from the Solway to parts of Wales, over the eastern counties for as far south as Suffolk, and while on passage in the area of the Tay. It often fails to reach its chosen haunts until the new year, although the first arrivals are usually made with the other grey geese in October. It is essentially a feeder on marsh grasses, although like other geese it is at times not particular. Gunners have noticed its unusual powers for taking evasive action at the moment it sees its enemy, and have remarked on its steep climb away from danger. The average weight of an adult is five pounds.

The bean goose is less common than any of the other three grey species, and generally speaking is confined to the southern half of the British Isles. Its chief haunts are in Ayr, Northumberland, Norfolk, and Suffolk, although elsewhere in goose country it is known as a passage migrant and a visitor in small numbers. It is recognisable by its orange beak with black nail, its dark head, brownish plumage, and orange feet. It is one of the few species to be found on inland waters and, equally, not to be found in the stubbles. Its favourite food is probably winter grass, but it has a partiality for clover and the leaves of young plants. Weight about six and a half pounds.

The brent and the barnacle are both little fellows, averaging in the neighbourhood of four pounds. I have shot a big mallard drake which was larger than a small brent. The main haunts of the barnacle are in the Hebrides and the Solway marshes, together with many parts of Ireland, while the brent are chiefly confined to the eastern sea-board from Northumberland, and in hard winters as far south as Kent, and round the south coast to Dorset. There are, however, two other forms of these birds—the dark and the pale breasted, the latter appearing in parts of Scotland and in Ireland. In appearance, the barnacle is very easy to identify through its startling contrasts of black, white, and grey plumage, with black feet. The brent is of a more uniform sooty black on top, with a dusky brownish under side.

DUCKS

One day, when leaning over the bridge which spans the lake in St. James's Park, I fell into conversation with a policeman. We talked about the ducks which were swimming below, trying to identify the species from our joint stock of meagre knowledge. The most surprising item of information which emerged was that my new friend had seen wild duck flight to the lake at dawn. They came in, he said, over the roofs of the Admiralty, circled briefly between the Mall and Queen Anne's Mansions, to make a good landing on the water at our feet. He thought they must have come from the lower reaches of the Thames Estuary.

For a creature bred in the wilds, it seemed strange to be told of its flight into the centre of the world's biggest city. I proposed to him that we should get up early the next morning to flight any further birds that came over the Admiralty building, a project which raised a smile, but no comments.

Whether wild duck do, in fact, flight into the centre of London I have no means of knowing, but it is certainly true that much of what I have written about the untamed independence of the species is, from time to time, set at naught by appearances such as these. The duck is not always wild. It is not invariably a bird which keeps its secrets to itself, to be encountered only in the empty places. Like other members of the wilderness, duck have acquired their shyness largely through persecution by mankind.

The class of shooting of which I have written is not connected with St. James's Park or any place where gentlemen have introduced duck for decoration or sport. It has been concerned solely with the hunting of the wild variety.

In this country there are some fourteen species with which the wildfowler may come in contact. They are divided equally into two classes — known as "surface" ducks and "diving" ducks. This is only a broad definition, and demands amplification to draw the distinctions more clearly.

The divers are short, tubby birds, with rather square wings, their feet set well back on their bodies, their flight a little laboured, in that the wing-beats are rapid, and their rise from the water is slow, like an under-powered aircraft. By comparison, the surface feeders are slenderly built, with lines which would appeal to an aircraft designer. Their aero-dynamic efficiency is almost certainly higher than that of the diving ducks, in that they can rise almost vertically off the water and fly with a comparatively slower rate of beat. They are also more comfortable on shore, walking with a measure of easy rhythm, in contrast to the waddle of the divers.

There are two other characteristics worth noting.

The first—a physical peculiarity—is the heavily webbed and lobed feet of all diving ducks, a characteristic explained by their under-water feeding habits. The second is the general practice of the divers to feed by day and the surface ducks by night.

The following list represents the species which are concerned :

Surface	Diving
Mallard	Pochard
Pintail	Tufted
Widgeon	Golden-eye
Shoveler	Scaup
Gadwall	Long-tailed
Garganey	Eider
Teal	Scoter

Of these, four may be disregarded, in that they are essentially sea-ducks, which rarely come inland during the winter and are consequently seldom encountered by the average wildfowler. They are, moreover, as uneatable as other mammals which subsist on a fish diet. They are the eider, scoter, scaup, and long-tailed ducks.

It is worth mentioning here that a hard winter will bring other species into the same gastronomical category, for, if they do not migrate further south, they are likely to seek the coast and the tidal reaches of the estuaries for their food, where the change of diet will soon give them the rank flavour common to mammals with a marine menu. Thus it is possible that a mallard, normally the most succulent of wild duck, may nauseate a wildfowler whose palate is otherwise numb.

One other species—the garganey—may also be deleted. It is essentially a summer resident which breeds in this country, but migrates to the south in the winter. Of the remainder, the mallard stands out above all the others. It not only breeds extensively in most parts of the British Isles, but its numbers are reinforced

by immigrants from Sweden, Finland, the Baltic
States, Denmark, Holland, and elsewhere. They pour
into our islands from the end of September, to distribute themselves on every type of water, large and
small. I have flushed them from the marshes of the
estuary, stalked them on the hill loch fifteen hundred
feet above sea-level and forty miles from the sea,
disturbed them on the banks of the stream, flighted
them along the shore, and hunted them among the
flooded willow thickets. From the haunts of the shy
trout in the southern chalk streams to the tawny pools
of the northern salmon rivers they have their being—
and high on the heather-covered slope, where the grouse
are nesting, I have met them conducting their broods
to the water. I have looked for them in the stubbles,
among the potatoes, and in the winter wheat. There
are few places where at some time of the year they are
not to be found. Not unnaturally, they form the major
part of a season's bag.

The mallard drake is a big fellow, weighing up to
as much as three pounds. His small dark green head,
white-ringed neck, and his back of mottled greys and
bronze make him instantly recognisable. The female is
a slightly smaller bird of soft speckled browns, her only
show of gaudiness lying in her wings, where the scapulars, like the drake's, glimmer with a steel-blue sheen.

The other ducks can perhaps be introduced most
conveniently through the following brief notes :

Pintail.—The colour of the drake is predominantly
grey, with white belly and dark chocolate-coloured
head, set on a slender neck. A recognition feature is
the long pointed tail. The female has the more sombre
aspect of the mallard duck. Breeds regularly in the
Loch Leven district, and elsewhere in Scotland more
sporadically. Its nest has, however, been recorded
in several English counties, although those birds
encountered by the wildfowler are more likely to be

winter visitors. As such, it is common, locally, on all
coasts, but is less often found in any numbers on inland
waters. Its flight is rapid, with quick wing-beats. In
character it is shy and suspicious. Food—chiefly
vegetable matter, including marine grasses, which spoil
its flavour for the table.

Widgeon.—A short-necked compact bird. The
general colour scheme of the drake is chestnut and grey,
with white belly, but the best recognition feature is its
yellow-buff forehead and the broad white patch which
extends inboard just behind the leading edge of its
wings. The female is brownish, also with a white belly,
but her most obvious feature is her remarkably short
and sharp-pointed bill.

Breeds extensively in Scotland, its range greatly
increased since it was introduced into Sutherland
a hundred years ago. Also a winter visitor on a large
scale. It loses much of its charm for the wildfowler
through its winter choice of marine food, for which it
haunts the estuaries, to the detriment of its flavour.
At the same time, it will visit the stubbles and the grass-
fields, and is to be found wintering on large sheets of
water—under which conditions its flavour becomes
excellent. I have often seen it resting on the sea in
flocks, and ornithologists have noted its instincts to
be markedly gregarious. The best chance of shooting
it is to wait at dusk, or in the moonlight by its feeding
ground on the flats.

Shoveler.—This duck is immediately recognisable
by its enormous bill, with which it justifies its name on
reedy meres, pools and muddy waters of no depth.
The drake has a dark green head, white breast and
scapulars, with chestnut belly and flanks, which are
unmistakable. The female is a sombrely dressed lady
not unlike the mallard duck, although her bill, together
with a short neck and heavy body, preclude any
possibility of confusion.

Breeds extensively all over the British Isles and appears to be increasing. The great majority which nest here, however, migrate in August and September, to be replaced by the winter visitors of the same species. Does not often resort to the sea, relying principally upon animal and vegetable matter from fresh water for its food.

Gadwall.—This is a difficult species to describe in a few words. The drake is a mixture of greys and browns, but perhaps the best recognition points are its generally speckled plumage, particularly about its head, dark grey bill and orange-yellow legs. Sits high on the water. The female is again reminiscent of the mallard duck, although she is smaller and more lightly built. Both birds have white bellies. Breeds regularly in Norfolk, Suffolk, and elsewhere in smaller numbers. Has a partiality for oats during the winter, although its chief diet is aquatic plants and seeds found in secluded meres, with an occasional change in the way of worms, frogs, and other animal matter.

Teal.—This is the smallest of the duck family, with the exception of the garganey. Anyone who has seen the lovely, swinging flight of a tight formation as it follows the course of a stream cannot mistake it. It is also probably the fastest of the species, attaining a speed of about a mile a minute over a short distance. Both male and female are immediately recognised by the brilliant metallic-green of the speculum, while other characteristics of the male are his spotted breast, greyish patterned back, and chestnut head, with a green band with buff edges outlining the eye. The colour scheme of the female is a mottled brown.

The teal breeds freely in most parts of the country, favouring rushy moorlands and heath pools. The visitors in winter are drawn generally from the coast of Europe from France to the Arctic Circle, and Iceland. Its feeding habits are similar to the mallard's, and during daylight they often share the same secluded pond.

DIVING DUCKS

Pochard.—This is a distinctive little duck. The drake is very easy to recognise by his chestnut-red head, black breast, and light grey back. The female is of a rather dull brown-grey, shading to an impure white on her under side. A strong characteristic, sooner or later noticed by the shooter, is a preference to swim to the middle of the water, out of range, instead of taking to the wing.

Breeds regularly in its favourite places from the north of Sutherland to the Thames Valley, chiefly down the east coast. Is fond of large sheets of open water during the winter, but seldom rests on the sea. Food—chiefly vegetable matter, for which it dives into shallow water. Principal hours of feeding are at dawn and dusk, and to a lesser extent at night.

Tufted Duck.—The startling contrast of the black-and-white plumage of the drake, together with its tuft, which grows out of the back of its head like a wisp of a boy's hair carelessly brushed, makes it instantly recognisable. The female, on the other hand, is of a fairly uniform dark brown, with a white belly which reaches far enough up the flanks to show when the bird is sitting on the water.

A noteworthy trait is its willingness to become domesticated when not disturbed, so that it is occasionally discovered as a visitor to the park pond. Its general habits are similar to the common pochard's, except for its special predilection for feeding on fish and spawn. It breeds extensively all over the British Isles, not excluding the north of Sutherland and the heel of Cornwall.

Golden-eye.—This is another black-and-white duck,

but the white predominates, while the black, glossy head has a bold white spot just below the eye. The female has a brownish head, with a thin white ring round its neck, and a mottled grey back. The neck appears to be very short in the air.

In habit it is much more of a sea-duck than either the tufted or the pochard, although a few winter on inland waters, particularly in Scotland. Like the pochard, it seems to prefer to swim to safety rather than fly, although when it decides to rise it does so more easily than the other divers. It is a great performer under water, obviously enjoying its submarine explorations. Its tastes in food are wide, although it is essentially an " animal " feeder, preferring crabs, shrimps, frogs, tadpoles, salmon spawn, and any sort of small fish.

It is a winter visitor and very rarely breeds in this country, although during the summer I have seen it many times in residence on Scottish lochs.

General.—The foregoing notes are concerned essentially with the habits and appearance of duck as they appear to the wildfowler during the winter months. In most species the drake is a far less colourful bird during the early summer. The changes after the moult are so great in some cases that a description of the full winter plumage would be unrecognisable for the same bird in July. The juvenile is, moreover, frequently incomplete in its plumage in many major respects.

No mention has been made, either here or in the text, of shelducks, goosanders, and mergansers. They are fish-eaters all, and generally reckoned to be unfit for human consumption. My only personal encounter at table with this triumvirate has been with the goosander—and it was a disaster. I shoot him whenever the opportunity offers because he is a far too successful trout fisherman.

PARTRIDGE

He is known as the common partridge, but he is only common as he displays gallantry in the face of adversity and love of family life, which are traits found in others who live under the same label. To have seen a pair sheltering their chicks in the height of a storm, while man and wife are battered almost into insensibility by hailstones, is to appreciate their devotion as parents ; or to watch a family party cross a road, the hen bird leading, and father following in the rear to hasten the stragglers, is to understand their intelligence. Of all game birds, they are the most virtuous and, when they come to their prime, the most sporting.

I have said something of their habits, but in so far as they can be protected and helped by ourselves during the breeding season the ensuing additional notes may be worth setting out.

The practice of building nests in hedgerows close to public roads is one which can be explained by the partridges' demand for " grit." It does not, however, take into consideration the danger from egg-collecting boys, and it is here that a poorly concealed nest can be made more secure with the help of dead branches and similar material, bearing in mind that dogs, as well as boys, go for walks along country roads. If the additional covering is added while the bird is still laying, and before she starts to sit (a period defined by her habit of covering the eggs with dried grass or leaves until her clutch is complete), there is little danger of causing the mother to desert.

Between nine and twenty eggs may be found in a nest from the middle of April onwards. During the first fortnight in May the partridge community is at its busiest. If there is wet, cold weather, flooding out the

home and destroying the eggs, the parents will start
again elsewhere, so that the chicks may not be hatched
until the end of June, or even later. During incubation
the hen never leaves the nest except for a brief period
at dawn and dusk, when she feeds. While she is away,
the cock will stand guard. During the incubation
period she must not be startled.

At between twenty-three and twenty-five days the
young will hatch, within a few hours of each other, and
as soon as they are dry, which is within an hour or two,
the brood will leave the nest, tended by both parents.
Any egg which is slow in hatching is left, so that
occasionally one will come across an unfortunate chick
which has broken out of its shell when the rest have
gone. Within ten days the chicks will be fluttering.
Within sixteen days they will be capable of flight. The
family will remain intact throughout the season unless
it is broken up by mortalities or wild weather. In an
open season it is common to see birds still together at
the beginning of February, when the cocks will be
thinking of taking wives. The previous year's families
are not broken up until this moment, and herein lies
a characteristic which will drive bereaved parents to
band together to form coveys of their own—a pathetic
effort at maintaining family life.

Flying characteristics need little amplification, except perhaps to remark that greater distances than a
mile are rarely flown at a time. If a covey has not been unduly startled, the birds will prefer to run rather than fly.
In the spring, when the parents are abroad with their
chicks, they are even more likely to crouch, teaching
their brood to do the same. There is sound sense in it,
for they are extremely difficult to see against their
natural background.

The feeding habit at dawn and dusk should be in-
violable. Not many shooters are abroad in the early
morning, but many prolong their sport into the hour

for feeding. There is no quicker method of driving the birds off the ground.

The red-legged or French partridge is common on many shoots, although it has been said that it mixes no better than rainbow and brown trout. As a generality, both presumptions are incorrect. The bird is a little larger than the common partridge, is more prone to run than fly, and when put up in a covey is likely to scatter. Unlike the common partridge, it will occasionally be seen perching on fences, in bushes, and even in trees. In appearance the birds are easily distinguished by their white cheeks and throat, and by their strongly barred flanks of black, white, and chestnut—in addition to their markedly red bill and legs. They are most sporting birds, often offering finer individual shots than the native breed. In general, their habits and behaviour are the same as our own stock, but during the nesting season the hen does not cover up her eggs, and there are fewer of them.

PHEASANT

There are a large number of varieties of this bird, and it would be true to say that the blood of the British stock is composed of most of them. It is for this reason that the plumage of individual specimens from the same area can differ widely. Basically, they are a species of long standing in England, possibly introduced by the Romans, but since then crossed with other imported breeds.

Compared with the domestic virtues of the partridge, the hen pheasant is a careless and rather stupid mother, full of good intentions, but lacking in many important qualities. As a father, the cock is a disgrace. He is polygamous to a high degree, and after the mating season, in March and April, takes no further interest in his family.

The hen scrapes a nest out of the ground under the cover of any type of herbage, lining it carelessly with dead leaves and a few stems of grass. There she will lay an average of fifteen eggs, and occasionally many more. If she succeeds in raising eight or nine poults under natural conditions, she is doing well. I have seen many instances of a bird failing to rear more than three or four. Apart from the ordinary hazards of the field, the young birds are singularly unintelligent, and will stray through thickets and dense cover, to lose themselves and perish. In extenuation of the mother's incompetence, it should be remembered that her family have not the benefit of a father's discipline.

If the first clutch of eggs is destroyed, or removed for artificial incubation, the hen will lay a second clutch of eight or nine eggs, provided the season is not too far advanced. She is not above doing this in another pheasant's nest.

The field characteristics need not be stressed again, except to repeat that the bird prefers to run for shelter rather than take flight. At the same time, no sportsman fails to appreciate the quality of his target once it is on the wing.

It can be recorded that damp places, such as rushy fields, reed, and sedge banks, are a strong favourite, both from the point of view of shelter and the food to be found in them.

GROUSE

The red grouse is essentially British. Its haunts are the native moorlands up to 2500 feet with occasional visits to the cultivated lowlands for feeding. It is thus that, occasionally, one may flush a covey in a field of stubble. Most of its food, however, consists of young heather shoots and bilberries.

It is said that a grouse will never perch on a wall,

a fence, or a tree. Notwithstanding this, there is a particular fence-post I know, which, for an unexplained reason, is a favourite of the local grouse. It has been the downfall of more than one bird when I have been out stalking. In severe weather, they are also capable of perching in bushes for the sake of their berries.

Apart from its susceptibility to disease, the bird is extraordinarily hardy, and so long as it can burrow down through the snow to obtain something to eat it can survive the hardest winter.

Mating takes place in March and by the end of April there should be many well-concealed nests among the heather. The number of eggs varies between six and eleven, occasionally more. The cock bird plays his part by remaining in the vicinity and, after the young are hatched, helping to guard them.

The flight is similar to other game birds and is not often sustained over any great distance. The rapid wing-beats alternating with long glides are characteristic.

The period during which the families will keep together is dependent chiefly upon the weather. More often than not, late September gales will break up the coveys and the grouse will pack, coming over the guns in clouds, and rendering shooting almost impossible. When packing occurs, it is equally difficult to walk up successfully, for the birds will rise at great distances, so that the shooter has little chance in any country except one which is broken up by hillocks and ravines.

RED DEER

Red deer have been known in the British Isles since the dawn of history. To-day they are confined to some three million acres of the Highlands, an area greater than it was a hundred years ago when the falling price of wool and mutton drove the flock masters from the

forests and left the higher glens deserted. Much of
the ground is as suited to the Blackface and Cheviot
sheep as it is to the deer, and the economy of the
approaching era is unlikely to ignore the fact.

The shooting season is elastic, in that deer are
not protected by the Game Laws. But tradition, which
is based on common sense, decrees that they shall be
shot only when they are in prime condition. This
automatically restricts the season for stags to some
six weeks—from the 20th of August to the 10th of
October. Hinds, on the other hand, are not shot until
much later, and then chiefly when it is desired to thin
the forest, kill off inferior beasts, or provide meat for
the larder.

In the spring of each year the stags cast their antlers
and start to grow a new set. By the end of July they
are usually fully grown and sharp-pointed, finally
hardening off in August. The early " velvet " glove
with which they are covered is stripped and discarded.
The quality of the antlers has been accepted during
the past hundred and fifty years as the yardstick to the
quality of the animal. Before that, its weight—which
may be anything up to twenty stones, and very occasionally more—was probably the prime consideration.
The qualities have little in common, for a stag with
a big spread and large number of points is less likely
to be heavy than another whose growth has made
flesh rather than horn. Each year the head will improve, until at the age of seven, eight, or nine it is likely
to be at its best. Although a beast may live to be twenty
or more, there are not many which escape the hazards
of the forest for more than a dozen years.

The preceding paragraphs are generalities, particularly as they relate to dates, for stags may come into
their prime throughout the stalking season. Thus, it is
possible that the same forest may show beasts in velvet
when others are " roaring." September 20th is,

however, the traditional day on which stags are said to enter the period of rut. Their voice in the forest as it echoes through the corries is an awe-inspiring sound. During the early part of October the rut is in full swing, and as every week of sexual excess goes by, so does the quality of the animal deteriorate.

From this moment, however, the hinds begin to improve in condition, until by December they are at their best. The calves will be dropped in May and June, and three years later the males will show signs of a head which will interest a stalker. Twins are a rarity, although cases are recorded from time to time. The hind never grows to the same size as the stag, and probably averages about eight stone.

As a race, the species are highly gregarious, and herds up to 3000 head have been recorded. In exceptionally hot weather, and likewise in times of great storms, the herds amalgamate for the enjoyment of the cool places and for shelter. As a generality, a stag gathers around him as large a harem as he can control. He will not be the only stag in the herd, but he will be the largest and most warlike, ever ready to beat off challengers and to employ the services of the younger stags as watchers against enemies.

I have already indicated their habits in earlier pages. It cannot, however, be said too often that they are influenced more than anything else by the wind. The nature of the beasts is to avoid all human contact, and, through a nose which is far more highly developed than any other sense, they rely on the wind for their safety and guidance. Thus a change of wind direction will often move the deer from one side of the forest to the other.

GLOSSARY OF TERMS

A CALF—a red deer's young from birth to weaning.

A HIND—a female red deer.

A HUMMEL—a mature stag which is hornless.

A STAG—a male red deer.

CLEAN (*adj.*)—referring to a stag that has got rid of his velvet.

RUT (*noun*)—the roar of the stag. Rutting is a loose term referring to the period of mating.

SWITCH—a stag with only brow points, four or five in all.

VELVET—a protective "fur" sheath enveloping the stag's horn while growing.

YELD (*adj.*)—or EILD (*Scot.*)—an eild hind is a female red deer not giving milk.

TABLES

The following tables may be found useful as providing additional information to that given in the two chapters on the choice of a gun. I have tried throughout to avoid technical material, not because it is without interest, but because it has been given elsewhere in greater detail and clarity than I could ever bring to it.

No. 1

No. of Gauge	Diameter of Bore in inches
4	1·052
8	·835
10	·775
12	·729
14	·693
16	·662
20	·615
28	·550

No. 2

THE NUMBERS OF PELLETS IN DIFFERENT CHARGES OF SHOT

Size of Shot	$1\frac{1}{8}$ oz.	$1\frac{1}{16}$ oz.	1 oz.
BB . . .	79	74	70
B . . .	90	85	80
1 . . .	113	106	100
2 . . .	135	127	120
3 . . .	158	149	140
4 . . .	191	181	170
$4\frac{1}{2}$ . . .	225	212	200
5 . . .	248	234	220
$5\frac{1}{2}$ . . .	270	255	240
6 . . .	304	287	270
$6\frac{1}{2}$ . . .	338	319	300
7 . . .	383	361	340
8 . . .	506	478	450
9 . . .	653	616	580
10 . . .	957	903	850

No. 3

DIAMETER OF SPREAD IN INCHES

Boring of Gun	Range in Yards						
	10	15	20	25	30	35	40
True cylinder	19	26	32	38	44	51	57
Improved cylinder . . .	15	20	26	32	38	44	51
Half choke	12	16	20	26	32	38	46
Full choke	9	12	16	21	26	32	40

Range in Yards	30	35	40	45	50	55	60
Percentage of 40-yards pattern in 30-inch circle	140	119	100	82	67	55	45

No. 4

Size of Shot	Minimum Effective Velocity in F.S.
A	215
BBB	222
BB	240
B	256
1	287
2	314
3	340
4	374
4½	406
5	426
5½	445
6	472
6½	496
7	529
8	609
9	690

No. 5

FORWARD ALLOWANCES IN FEET FOR STANDARD CARTRIDGE

Range in Yards	Bird crossing at 40 m.p.h.	Bird crossing at 60 m.p.h.
20	3·7	5·5
25	4·7	7·1
30	5·9	8·8
35	7·7	10·7
40	8·5	12·7
45	10·0	14·9
50	11·6	17·4
60	15·0	22·0

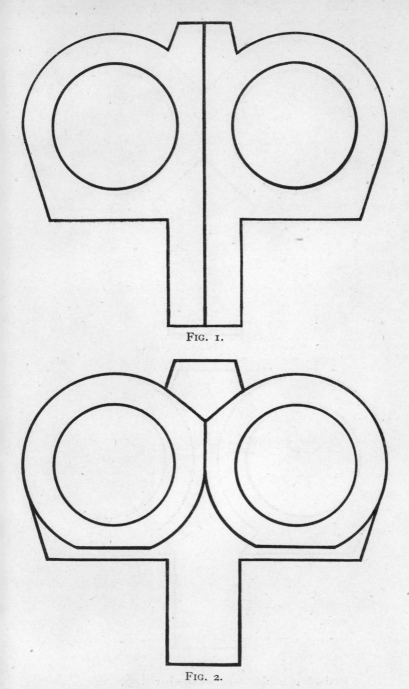

Fig. 1.

Fig. 2.

Methods of joining together two barrels (*see page* 84).

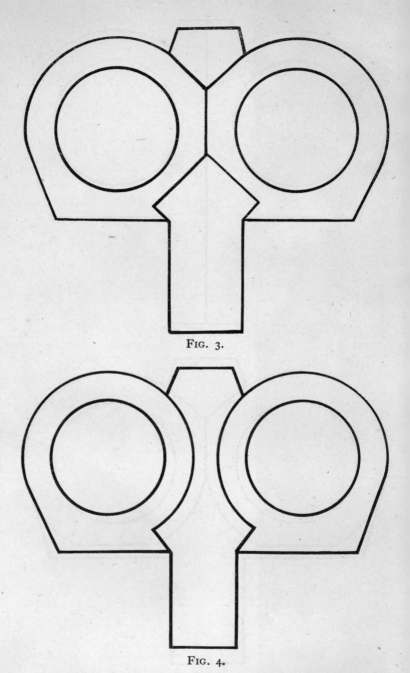

FIG. 3.

FIG. 4.

Methods of joining together two barrels (*see page* 84).